# SUMMER CIRCUIT

Also by Kim Ablon Whitney

*The Perfect Distance*
*Blue Ribbons*

# Summer
# CIRCUIT

## Kim Ablon Whitney

ISBN-10: 0692382887

Cover by Littera Designs
Interior design by Anne Honeywood
Cover photos by Caranine Smith/Bigeq.com and
©iStock.com/EricFerguson
Text set in Sabon

*for Liz Benney—a fellow writer, my riding fairy godmother, and a great friend*

# Chapter 1

THERE ARE TIMES IN YOUR LIFE when things change completely. I don't think this happens in everyone's life because not everyone lives a part of their life as one person and then discovers that they can live another part of their life as another person. Not that I truly became another person. Maybe I just discovered myself in that adolescent way people are supposed to discover themselves. But one thing is for sure, when I pulled into the show grounds on July third, I had no idea everything was about to change.

* * *

Mrs. Gorham drove the trailer. I followed behind, going fifty-five on the highway and then plugging along at thirty up the winding mountain roads in Vermont. It was awful driving behind a trailer. I couldn't see anything except the back of the ramp and the words CAUTION: HORSES! Even though I knew I wouldn't be passing the trailer for the whole four hours, I couldn't help weaving to catch a glimpse of the road ahead.

The rest of the time I looked at the passing scenery as we traveled through tiny rural towns with improbable names like Harmonyville, Athens, and Jamaica. For a while the road paralleled the river and every now and then there would be a covered bridge or swimming spot with cars parked alongside it.

We passed old white farmhouses, their pretty porches dotted with rocking chairs and decorated with American flags for the Fourth of July. Belted Galloway cows, reminding me of giant Oreo cookies, grazed in pastures next to the farmhouses. There were tumbledown houses too—holes in their roofs, windows long boarded up.

When we finally pulled into the dirt driveway of the horse show, my stomach started twisting. Trailers were everywhere, two-horse trailers like Mrs. Gorham's, six-horse goosenecks, and huge sixteen-horse rigs. Grooms, calling to each other mostly in Portuguese, unloaded horses, their legs wrapped in farm colors.

"So this is a big deal hunter/jumper show," Mrs. Gorham said.

"Well, there are bigger deal shows than this," I said.

The horses from my trainer's barn were coming directly from another big show that they'd been at for two weeks. It hadn't been easy for my trainer to find my horse a ride to Vermont, but she'd finally found Mrs. Gorham, a woman who rode dressage at a nearby barn.

"And you really stay here for seven straight weeks?"

"I guess it's different than the dressage world," I said.

"You can say that again," she said. "Well, let's start unloading."

I was still looking around the grounds, shielding the sun from my eyes with my hand, even though I had sunglasses on. High school was over. No looking back. There was college to look forward to, but before that, there was the summer circuit. Seven whole weeks in Vermont horse showing without my mom or dad.

My mom was terrified of what that would mean and whether I would be able to survive on my own. My dad probably was too, but he'd been the one to decide this was just what I needed. He had a sink-or-swim plan to make me able to fend for myself—drop me at the horse show for seven weeks without a groom. I'd be taking care of Logan all by myself when I'd hardly so much as picked up a brush or a pitchfork in my years of riding.

We consulted the stall chart by the feed and bedding office and found my stalls, in the aisle next to the stalls of my trainer, and unloaded Logan. He nearly catapulted himself backwards off the trailer, snorted and looked around, his head high and neck muscles tight.

"I better lead him in," Mrs. Gorham said, putting the chain over his nose.

When I just stood there, she jutted her chin to the trailer. "Grab a bale of hay. All this stuff has to go in."

I'd never carried a bale of hay and it was surprisingly heavy and awkward. I wobbled toward the tent, the bale bouncing off my thighs, and the twine digging into my fingers. I dropped it twice and finally stumbled into the aisle.

Mrs. Gorham helped me carry in everything else. My trunk, another bale of hay, five bags of shavings, Logan's feed, muck bucket and pitchfork, water and feed buckets, and tool-box. I took the light things like the buckets while stout Mrs. Gorham hoisted shavings bags onto her shoulder, carrying the pitchfork with her free hand. She maneuvered my tack trunk onto a hand-truck and wheeled it smoothly over the bumps and divots in the ground.

I sat down on a bale of hay, sweaty and already ex-hausted. Logan nosed around in the stall behind me, plucking up the grass over which the tent had been set up.

"Okay." Mrs. Gorham dusted off her hands. "Have a good summer!"

I looked up at her. "Wait, aren't you going to set up?"

She took a step backward. "I'm on strict instructions . . ." She hesitated, as if she were maybe considering helping me out even if my dad had told her to dump my stuff and run. She was probably concerned for Logan more than she was for me. But before she could change her mind, she turned and left. I guess I could have chased after her and begged, but I was too busy being pissed at my dad. He was a self-made man. An entrepreneur who'd dropped out of college and started a company that sold for millions. Given his money, though, he didn't live an incredibly lavish lifestyle. He and his second wife, Monica, lived in a spacious, but by no means grand, house in Palo Alto. Mom got her share of his millions in the divorce and she and I lived a comfortable life devoid of any material wants in a Boston suburb. Mom didn't work—but that was a whole other story. My dad liked people who worked hard. Monica was an executive vice president of a software firm herself. Dad hated that Mom didn't work and he hated that she'd babied me. My older brother Ryan was just like Dad. He was a sophomore at Stanford and he'd already founded two companies that were doing pretty well. Seriously. *Two* companies. It was a good thing I loved my brother, or I would have totally hated him. I wasn't a total deadbeat. I got good grades and was headed to Tufts. But I never did anything amazing, not like Dad or Ryan. And Dad thought I wasn't ready for the real life of college. He wanted me to learn responsibility, perseverance, and hard work.

Logan sneezed behind me, startling me. I turned to look at him. I couldn't just leave him in the stall without bedding, hay, or water. No matter how much I resented Dad for trying to make me into something he wanted me to be, I had a fifteen-hundred pound animal depending on me. I surveyed the aisle filled with buckets, shavings and feed bags, and hay bales. I had my work cut out for me. I stood up, sparked by the idea that this was some kind of test Dad had orchestrated. SURVIVOR: Horse Show.

I would so prove him wrong.

# Chapter 2

I HAULED THE BAGS OF SHAVINGS into Logan's stall, but somehow I couldn't figure out how to open them. I clawed at the thick plastic, but my non-existent nails were useless. I finally opened up a pathetic, tiny hole and tore from there. I took my anger out on the plastic, tearing it into shreds. For the next bags, I decided to use scissors from the tool box to get the bags started. It was amazing how much easier that went. Once all the shavings were down, I realized I'd lost track of all the pieces of plastic from the first bag I'd ripped apart.

"Crap!"

I couldn't just leave them there, buried in the shavings. If by mistake Logan ate one, he could choke and die or it could clog up his stomach. I found a few pieces, but how many had I torn off in my frustration? I certainly hadn't kept count. Four? Six? Eight? I bent over, searching the shavings. Logan looked at me like I was crazy, pawing around by his feet. He put his nose next to my face and blew, tickling my ear.

"You're lucky I'm even looking for these," I told him.

Logan bordered on disaster-horse and although I often said things like "I want to kill you" in my head when I rode him, I didn't *actually* want him dead. I could just see Dad getting the call that on my first day at the show I'd managed to kill Logan. Logan kept following me, brushing my neck with his nose like he might find a treat there. It was kind of cute and endearing—until he sneezed again, covering my neck and the side of my face with gooey horse snot.

"Gross! Really?" I said, turning to look at him as I wiped the snot off my face.

He took a step back like he was saying, "Who? Me?"

After ten minutes of looking and seriously considering giving up and hoping for the best, I had found six shreds of plastic and I had gone through what seemed like every last shaving. I would have to just hope that I'd found all the plastic. Logan was still looking at me like I was crazy. Clearly no one had ever had this much trouble making up his bed.

I threw the plastic bags over the stall door and kicked the shavings to spread them. I was wearing shorts and espadrilles and when I was done my shoes and legs were covered in itchy shaving dust. Apparently, jeans and paddock boots would have been a better choice.

I took the empty bags outside to the trash can. Leftover shavings I hadn't dumped out of the bags flew up in my face, covering my skin and hair and going up my nose. It was entirely disgusting. I stood by the trash barrel, coughing and sputtering, and trying to stuff the bags into the already full barrel, as a groom I recognized from my trainer's barn came out with empty shavings bags. His bags were somehow folded and stuffed into each other, as neat and compact as origami.

"You can just leave them next to the barrel." He deposited his own stash there. "They'll come around and pick them up later." He was one of the more experienced grooms, one of those in charge at Jamie's barn, but I couldn't remember his name.

"Oh, okay." I wiped my face, trying to get off the shavings that I was sure were stuck there. "Thanks."

He looked at me a moment longer, clearly amused by seeing one of the clients having to get her hands dirty and doing a bad job of it at that.

Jamie, my trainer (I used the term loosely because the word trainer implied that she imparted knowledge), met me on my way back. "Hannah, when did you get here?"

"A little while ago."

Jamie was wearing her usual—jeans and a polo shirt. She never wore shorts, ever. Not on the hottest day possible. Her dyed red hair was pulled back in a tight ponytail.

"Well, you better get on and get in the ring. As soon as you can. We've got our work cut out for us this summer." She cocked her head at me. "What happened to you anyway? Your hair is covered in shavings."

"Uh, just, nothing."

Jamie raised her eyebrows at me and walked away. She could have asked if I needed help, which it was pretty obvious I did. But Dad had probably gotten to her too.

I rushed through the rest of the set-up since Jamie wanted me on Logan. I wasn't sure how to hang the water buckets in the stall and no one else was in the aisle yet for me to look at how they had done it. It was one of those things I'd just never noticed before. Buckets always seemed to be magically hanging in the stalls. Or actually I'm not sure I'd ever really spent any time in Logan's stall at a show. He was always tacked up and put away for me.

I didn't have time to waste so I just decided I would put them on the ground for now. I took the two buckets and filled them at the wash rack. They were so heavy and I'd filled them nearly to the brim so the water sloshed out all over my legs as I lugged them in. Once the buckets were there, they looked completely wrong. Logan had to lower his head nearly to his ankles to drink. He took a sip and then gave me that "you're nuts" look again. I'd figure out where they really went later. Jamie would kill me if I wasn't on soon and I still had to get dressed, groom Logan, and get him tacked up.

I decided I'd get dressed first, which turned out to be a bad idea. By the time Logan was tacked up, my breeches were gross and my polo shirt stained and sweaty. I led Logan outside and realized there was no groom to give me a leg up. I pulled down my stirrup and put my toe in the iron. I went to hoist myself up and my saddle literally swung down Logan's side. Apparently I hadn't tightened my girth enough. Could I do anything right? I looked around, sure people were pointing and laughing, but thankfully everyone was busy going about their own business. I undid the girth, repositioned the saddle and did up the girth extra tight. Somehow I managed to just barely pull myself into the saddle as Logan took off at an extended walk toward the rings.

# Chapter 3

"HANNAH!" JAMIE YELLED. "Get in here!"

I legged Logan forward, but he didn't budge. After sprinting to the ring, he was now frozen solid. Tuesday was warm-up day. In addition to being the day everybody spent unpacking, it was the day all the riders practiced before the competition began the next day. That meant the ring was teeming with riders.

"Kick him!" Jamie yelled.

I kicked him and we were in the ring. I felt a rush of air as a girl who looked clean and composed cantered by.

"Get to the trot if you don't want to get killed out here!" Jamie called over the voices of the other trainers.

Logan immediately surged forward to a racing trot. I knew I was in trouble. I should have spent the day getting him acclimated. Taking it easy. But Jamie never wanted things easy. Logan's trot was wild, and every few strides he would throw his head.

"How's he feel?" Jamie asked.

"Fresh," I said. Understatement of the century.

"Keep working while I help Maddie. I'll be with you in a few minutes."

If I lived that long.

I made it twice around the ring before I saw someone coming straight for us. It was Logan's least favorite thing, his very own pet peeve. When someone came at him from the other direction, he freaked out, usually grabbing the bit and running. Even though I knew I had to stay calm so he stayed calm, I couldn't help it. My knees clenched around the saddle. My hands tightened on the reins. The rider coming at me was going to stay to the inside of the ring; I would pass on the outside. As we came closer to each other, I held my breath. Please, please, please let Logan not freak out.

Logan tossed his head vigorously and scooted a bit to the left, but that was minor for him. It seemed as if we had actually survived. Maybe Logan was going to surprise me and turn over a new leaf this summer. No more Black Stallion imitations. I put my reins in one hand to pat him and that's when it all went wrong.

I looked up and he was coming at me at a canter.

"Outside," he said, which meant I should move to the inside. Left shoulder to left shoulder. Pass left to left like when driving, that's what I had always learned. But he was approaching fast and wanted the outside, even though I was obviously in his way.

"Outside!" he said again, this time louder and with urgency.

My arms stiffened. I grabbed the left rein and pulled,

trying to steer Logan to the inside of the ring and let him pass on the outside, but instead Logan leapt up in the air, full-mechanical-bull-imitation, and surged to the right, directly into the path of the oncoming horse.

The guy pulled his horse up hard and we both stopped, head on, inches from each other. For extra points, Logan snorted and pawed out at the other horse.

I looked up, cringing.

"I said outside," the other rider said.

I hardly knew anyone on the show circuit, but the guy looking at me from atop his big bay warmblood looked vaguely familiar. For one thing, he was incredibly hot. The horse show world was low on guys to begin with and so the ones who rated high on the hot scale stood out. Frankly, even unattractive guys became appealing in the horse show world. An actual attractive straight male was like the Holy Grail. Even the attractive gay guys warranted regretful sighs and sometimes even failed attempts to change their sexual orientation.

"Sorry," I murmured.

His brown eyes softened slightly. "Next time watch where you're going."

He steered his horse to the right and departed straight away into a canter. I heard Jamie's voice from across the ring.

"Hannah!" Jamie pointed to the in-gate, which I'd only just entered. "Get that horse out of here. Take him outside for a hack."

Jamie was shaking her head. I moved Logan, whose neck was covered with sweat and was blowing hard even though we had barely trotted, toward the in-gate. Behind me I heard Jamie say, "Sorry, Chris. You know how some of them can be."

I didn't think about what Jamie had just implied about me. Instead I ran his name through my head. Chris. Chris. Chris . . . Kern? My face flushed red. I remembered his photo and the article I'd read about how he had won the grand prix at Devon.

Could I really have crashed into Chris Kern?

# Chapter 4

I WALKED LOGAN AROUND the show grounds, making sure to stick to the paths labeled HORSES ONLY and not find myself on the paths marked for dirt bikes and golf carts. That was just what I didn't need—to crash into a moving vehicle after already crashing into the show's top rider. Logan refused to calm down, jigging and chewing the bit the whole time. I finally gave up and took him back to the barn. I stripped off his tack and threw him in the stall. I glanced at the water buckets on the ground and the mountains of shavings now mixed with dirt, since Logan had dug around to forage for the grass underneath. I quickly retreated to my tack trunk and hung my head in my hands. This was beyond a disaster.

"He-llo!"

I heard Zoe's voice and looked up to see her and Jed walking into the aisle.

"We heard you crashed into Chris Kern!" Zoe said and Jed quickly added, "Something I've always aspired to do myself."

Zoe gave Jed a fake-disgusted look and directed her gaze back to me. "You've been here, what, a few hours? And you're already getting into trouble?"

"How did you know?" I'm sure my face showed my horror. "Did you see it?"

Zoe chuckled. "Word travels. What did he say?"

I lowered my voice to imitate Chris. "Watch where you're going next time."

"That sounds like Chris—über-serious. So, what's Jamie having you do this summer?"

"Children's jumpers. You know, stick with the low fences so I don't kill myself."

Most juniors in their last year were doing the big eq, junior hunters, or junior jumpers, or a combination of all three. That's what Jed and Zoe were doing. But they weren't tragic-junior-rider me.

"How's Logan anyway?" Zoe wandered over to peer into his stall. "What the—?"

Jed joined her and soon both of them were staring at the mess I'd made. Logan had knocked one of the buckets over, probably on purpose, creating a big circle of wet shavings.

"I'm not sure what looks worse, this stall or you," Zoe said. "You put the water buckets on the ground?"

Jed shivered. "Extreme *un*makeover."

"I wasn't sure how to hang them."

"Did you try the hooks?" Zoe motioned to two lovely metal circles on the side of the stall, right there to attach a double-ended clip to. How had I missed those?

"I guess I didn't see them," I mumbled.

Zoe stepped closer to me. "And is that dirt on your neck? How did you get dirt on your *neck*?"

"This whole thing was kind of a challenge."

"I see that."

I hung my head again. Zoe and Jed had ridden with Jamie much longer than I had, since they had been doing the ponies. They had spent years on the road together, riding in six o'clock lessons, finishing first and second in the same classes, staying at the same hotels. They were always super nice to me, but I wasn't one of them.

"Oh, honey," Zoe said. "Don't cry. Is she crying?"

"I don't know, maybe," Jed said.

"I'm not crying," I muttered.

Zoe came to sit on one side of me on the tack trunk. "Who's taking care of Logan? Pablo? Why didn't he set up your stalls?"

"*I'm* taking care of Logan."

"By yourself?" Zoe's eyes went wide.

I nodded.

Jed gasped. "Why? Did your dad go bankrupt, or go to prison for insider trading or something?"

Zoe shot Jed a look. "Manners, Jed."

"What? It happened to Amanda Connors. She's down to *two* horses."

"My dad didn't go bankrupt. He wants me to suffer. I mean, learn to be independent."

Jed slid onto the tack trunk on the other side of me. "We'll help you."

"Do you even know how to set up a stall?" I asked.

Jed grinned. "No, but Zoe does."

Zoe liked to pretend she was one of the juniors with tons of money. Really, she was the daughter of a small-time professional who bought and sold horses in Virginia. She had grown up doing all her own work, even if now most of the time Jamie gave her grooms.

Zoe stood up. "First thing we have to do is hang your buckets. That's like a tragedy waiting to happen in there."

We put Logan in the grooming stall and Zoe and Jed helped me. We clipped the buckets onto the hooks. Jed dragged the hose in to fill the buckets as Zoe showed me how to bank the shavings to the sides.

She wielded the pitchfork expertly, like some girls used a round brush and a blow-dryer. "Leave it banked so Logan can eat whatever grass is left and then later this afternoon pull some shavings down, but not all of them."

While we were working, one of the grooms from Jamie's barn, Mike, came over to find Zoe. "Jamie says you need to get on Baxter."

Mike was one of the few white grooms and he stuck out in his tank top and black jeans. He rode a motorcycle and was into weight-lifting, He was the last person you would ever imagine working with horses. He also was totally into Zoe. He was only a few years older than us. He hadn't gone to college and might not have even graduated from high school. Zoe liked to flirt with him sometimes because he wasn't ugly and he was really nice, but she'd never be with him, she'd said, not even for a one-night stand.

"I'm helping Hannah set up," Zoe told him.

"You can help me after," I said.

Zoe gave Mike a trying-to-be-cute smile. "Unless you have time after you get Baxter ready for me . . ."

Her smile worked. Mike made a show of acting kind of put-out, but I knew he loved the idea of helping Zoe, even if it meant helping me. "Okay," he said. "But you owe me."

"Maybe," Zoe said. "What do you have in mind?"

"A drink at Backcountry."

"I could do that," Zoe said.

It was agreed. Mike got Zoe on Baxter and then he came back and helped me finish Logan's stall and get the grooming stall up. In minutes he had the rubber mat down on the floor and the brush box positioned. In the third stall he put my feed, extra hay bales, supplements, muck bucket, pitchfork, and rake. I watched him, trying to learn how it was all done in case I ever had to do it again.

When it was all set he brushed his hands off on his jeans.

"Thank you so much," I said.

"Anytime. You going to come out for a drink?"

I shrugged. "I don't know. Maybe. Are you going tonight?"

"Nah, probably Sunday . . . that's the real party day."

I nodded. I'd often heard the whispers about Sunday nights. "We'll see," I said.

"You're going to have fun up here," Mike said. "Everyone does."

I thought back to my day so far. Crashing into Chris, botching my stall set-up. It had to get better than this.

# Chapter 5

JAMIE SAID SHE WOULD GIVE me a lesson on Wednesday morning and then I would show in a 1.00 meter class that afternoon. I didn't feel at all ready, but I didn't have any say in things like that. Jamie reigned supreme. She was a dictator and even the parents kowtowed to her. Most outsiders to the sport would never understand why people paid gobs of money to be treated like dirt by a trainer with dyed red hair who said, "idear," instead of "idea." But where we lived on the South Shore there were few A-level barns and once you started riding with a trainer, it was hard to leave, unless you were one of those fickle people who hopped trainers every few months. Even though Jamie was mean and often not very helpful, riding with her became familiar and it was hard to break those ties.

Early Wednesday morning, I went to put Logan on the cross-ties so I could clean his stall. I decided I would start with emptying his water buckets. I went to unhook them and what did I find? Poop. Floating horse poop. He had pooped in his bucket. How did a horse even pull that off? I had never seen it before, or even known it was a thing horses did. And what kind of sick horse would crap in his own water? I gave Logan a sidelong look and then dragged the buckets outside, unsure whether to dump them in the wash stall or the manure pile. Mike was dumping a wheelbarrow and saw me staring into the bucket.

"What you got in there?" he asked. "The fountain of youth?"

"No, manure."

Mike nodded. "A floater."

"So this is like a thing?" I said. "My horse isn't the first to invent this little demented trick?"

"Nah, some horses do it."

"Why?"

Mike shrugged. "Scrub it extra good. You showing today?"

"Yup." I had the feeling my day wouldn't be getting much better.

* * *

The minute I entered the ring for my class, I felt like someone was watching me. And I didn't mean Jamie, because she hardly ever gave me her full attention. While I was on course, she was always checking her phone or calling back to the barn on her walkie-talkie.

I wanted to look around at the few people in the stands and alongside the ring, but I knew looking anywhere but straight down the middle of Logan's ears would only do two things—make Jamie scream at me and probably make me go off course.

I heard the electronic beep signaling that the timer was reset and that I could start my course. One last time, I retraced my path in my mind. Starting over the single oxer, left turn to the four-stride line on the outside, then sit up, collect, balance for the vertical on the corner, go forward a little to the oxer-vertical across the diagonal, turn right to the two-stride on the far outside and then regroup for the finish over the tight five. That is, if I even got over fence number one. Logan had been terrible in my lesson, stopping multiple times, but here I was still going in the ring.

I squeezed Logan into a canter. It sounded so straightforward going over it in my head. That was the easy part. I could hear Jamie's last instruction to me. *Press him forward. Don't be indecisive. Give him a good ride.* I clucked to Logan to lengthen his stride and then sat back in the saddle and tried to relax. Jamie hadn't exactly mentioned anything about relaxing on course, but I knew that practically hyperventilating like I usually did would certainly prevent me from thinking clearly. Then again, relaxing on course was not something I had quite yet mastered. Relax, I told myself, relax.

On the approach to the first jump, a red oxer, I realized that the reason why I couldn't relax was because I knew something was bound to go wrong. My stomach was spinning and I could feel Logan tense up through his neck and his back until he felt ten inches shorter in length and five inches taller in height than he had when we had entered the ring. He snatched at the bit, making me brace against him, my back rigid. I leaned back in the saddle and tried at the same time to put my leg firmly against his side so he would know I wanted him to go. As I turned the corner to the oxer, Logan tossed his head into the air, loosening my grip on the reins. I tried to quickly gather up my reins again and to kick Logan forward to the jump. He propped a few short strides, stopped dead and wheeled around on his hind legs back toward the in-gate.

I let out a quiet groan. We hadn't even gotten within ten strides of the first jump and Logan had already decided he wouldn't go.

"Hit him!" Jamie screamed from the in-gate.

I looked at Jamie, then at Logan, and then down at my hands. I didn't have a crop to hit him with. That was something a groom might have reminded me to carry, but of course I had gotten myself on and up to the ring. It was a miracle the tack was even on right. Something had felt like it was missing when I tacked up—I guess it was the crop that a groom always handed me.

"Use your hand, the slack of your reins," Jamie yelled. "Hit him!"

I looked at Jamie again and then kicked Logan. My calf hit his side and Logan didn't even flinch. I kicked harder and this time it was enough to spark Logan into a canter. I headed to the oxer again. By now, Logan was covered with a frothy sweat and was grinding his teeth on his bit so much the metal was squeaking. I braced back in the saddle again, silently praying that this time he would jump. Logan lunged at the fence as if he was going to go, then changed his mind, sliding to a stop at the base of the jump and taking the first few rails down. I was thrown forward slightly onto his neck by the stop, and had to crawl back into the saddle.

"Thank you in Jumper II," the announcer boomed over the loud speaker, making sure I wouldn't go rogue and keep trying to jump the course. It was a phrase I had heard countless times before. Two refusals and you were out. How I longed for the days before FEI rules when I would at least get three shots at making it over.

The one good thing, I thought to myself, was that I didn't even feel like crying anymore, which was what I'd done practically every time I'd shown Logan when I'd first gotten him.

Before Logan, I'd leased a wonderful horse from a girl who had ridden with Jamie, and then went to college and was too busy to ride. Dobby was nineteen and had done and seen it all. He'd done the hunters and the eq finals but couldn't jump over three feet anymore. He never stopped at a fence, no matter what hideous distance I got him to. Somehow he'd find a way to get over and make it look halfway okay. He was never quick or worried. He was a complete saint and I loved him. Back then, I liked riding too. I'd never been good at any other typical sports like soccer or basketball, and while I wasn't great at riding by any stretch, Dobby made me feel like I was mildly competent. It also got me out of the house and away from Mom. We had been talking about buying a horse and then Dobby's owner graduated, got a job on the West Coast, and decided to retire Dobby to a farm down South.

Instead of going horse-shopping in Europe with Jamie like most people at the barn did—where Jamie would pick out an appropriate horse—my dad had bought Logan on a total whim. He'd had a business dinner with a man who it turned out bred his own warmbloods in California. The man had raved to Dad about all the great jumper prospects he had. After too many glasses of expensive wine, Dad had agreed to buy a certain prospect that the man was telling him about. By the time Dad told me, the money had already been wired and Logan was on his way across the country to Jamie's barn. Dad had even named him for me—*Personal Best*. Of course Dad had picked that name. Logan was pretty to look at, with his dark bay coat and white socks on all four feet, but it was clear he was much greener than the man had indicated. Logan was way too much horse for me. Jamie tried to tell Dad as much, but he simply told her to "make it work." If it was up to Dad, I might have switched trainers. He wasn't the type to kowtow to anyone. But it was always Mom who said we should just stay with Jamie. She hated change of any kind, even if it was for the ultimate best. A year after we'd gotten Logan, it still wasn't working.

In the beginning I'd felt pretty sorry for myself. I mean who else had a dad stupid enough to buy a horse without even looking at it? A dad who had never ridden a day in his life except for the odd vacation trail ride? Now I was basically resigned to the fact that Logan was a psycho. In all honesty, I'm not sure I would've known what to do if he had jumped around the course.

While the jump crew reset the jump, I left the ring at the trot, Logan going more sideways than forward. I kept my head down. At the in-gate, Jamie was waiting, arms crossed.

"What were you doing out there?"

"I . . ."

"Nothing," Jamie said, "You're sitting on top of that horse like a sack of potatoes waiting for him to march you around. Well, I have news for you, it's not going to happen. Not today and not by the end of the summer."

I nodded weakly.

"This horse is not going to cart you around and until you learn that you might as well give up, which is what you're doing anyway."

"I know."

"And besides your stick, you forgot to put on his running martingale."

So that was the tangle of leather still in my trunk. I wasn't sure I could have put it on right even if I had realized what it was.

Jamie paused and glared at me. I glanced away from her stare at the sidelines of the ring. Chris was standing with his back to the ring, looking straight at me.

# Chapter 6

NOT ONLY HAD CHRIS SEEN my awful ride, but he was close enough to hear Jamie yelling at me. Actually, anyone within a hundred-foot radius of the in-gate heard her.

She continued her attack on me, mixing outrage with pure despair. "You're going to have to do better than this. What the hell were you thinking?"

When I didn't answer, my mind still on Chris, she snapped, "Answer me so I know someone's in there and you're not brain dead!"

"I don't know what I was thinking," I managed. "I was just trying to get him over the jumps."

"*That* was trying to get him over the jumps?"

"I guess so, yeah."

Jamie shook her head like she'd just witnessed the fall of civilization, and turned away.

I knew Logan wasn't push-button and wouldn't just cart me around, but couldn't he at least jump the jumps? Was that too much to ask? I didn't plan to go out there and be terrible. But Jamie didn't see it that way. She saw it all as my fault.

I wanted to hate Logan completely, but it wasn't entirely his fault either. We were a bad match, never meant to be.

As I headed to the barn, I glanced back to see a new rider on course, cantering the jumps flawlessly. Chris was still by the ring. It looked like he was watching me although I was too far away to tell for sure and why would he be watching me anyway? He must have had some other reason to be at the jumper ring.

Logan race-walked the whole way back to the barn, his head and shoulders lurching. I tried to slow him, but he only walked faster. When I got to the barn, I stopped him a few feet from the tent and jumped off. I wanted to throw him at a groom and go back to the condo I was staying in, but of course there was no groom to throw him at. I was stuck putting him away myself. I took off his tack and grabbed my wash bucket. I took him out to the wash area and turned the hose on him. He danced around as I sprayed him, nearly stepping on my toes.

"Stand still!" I commanded, but he backed up, pulling on the lead rope. I gave him a hard tug and told him again that he better stand still. I pointed the hose at his chest and sprayed. He swung around quickly, dodging the spray, and in the process knocked over the bucket I'd filled with liniment. I reached down to grab the bucket and he pulled back again, this time knocking the hose out of my hand. It landed a foot away and the spray nozzle hit the ground, turning it on and spraying me all over. It was wriggling like a snake, spraying everything. I was soaked; Logan was freaking out. I somehow managed to grab the rogue hose and turn off the sprayer while barely holding on to Logan. I took a deep breath and looked over to see Mike chuckling at me.

"Never good to battle the hose," he said. "The hose always wins."

I wiped back my drenched hair. I knew I looked like I'd just stepped out of the shower, only clothed. "He won't stand still."

Mike was holding a chestnut horse and a bucket like mine. He put the bucket down. "Watch and learn." He started out by gently spraying the horse's legs. "You have to get them acclimated. Would you like a shower all of a sudden?"

"No," I said. I'd just had one and it hadn't felt good.

"First the legs, then the chest, neck, and hind-end. Then the back and stomach. Those are the most sensitive parts."

His horse stood still, looking as if he was even enjoying the wash-down. Mike finished by sponging his head. "Never spray close to the head or ears. Most horses hate that. Some people do it anyway, but they're cruel."

"You're really good with horses," I told him. I didn't add that no one would ever expect burly Motorcycle Mike to do anything with animals except maybe leave them behind as road kill.

"Your turn," Mike said. "Start with his legs—from the knee down."

Mike supervised, instructing and encouraging me as I went. Logan didn't exactly stand still—this was Logan—but it went much better. Mike even watched me use the sweat scraper, telling me to be gentle on Logan's stomach. "He's a horse, not a car. Now take him in and dry off his legs real good with a towel so he doesn't get rain rot."

"What's rain rot?"

"A skin infection. It's gross. All their hair falls out. You don't want him to get it."

Mike started leading the chestnut back to the barn.

"Thanks!" I called after him.

# Chapter 7

I SHOWED LOGAN IN THE 1.00 meter class again on Thursday and then in the children's jumpers on Friday, Saturday, and Sunday. Sunday I realized I didn't have any clean saddle pads and had to use a filthy one. Not a good start to the day. How had I not realized all my laundry was dirty and taken it to the horse-laundry truck?

In total, I made it over jumps in four days. Mostly I listened to Jamie find new ways to insult me ringside. At night, I holed up in my condo feeling lonely and sorry for myself. To make matters worse, there seemed to be fireworks each night, including on the Fourth. Every time I saw a spark of light or heard a boom, I pictured people out having fun together and celebrating, while I was by myself.

On Sunday, I was back in the tent after my round when Zoe came into the aisle. I'd heard her name announced all day. She was small junior hunter champion, large junior hunter champion, and won the high junior jumper classic.

"Wanna go out tonight?" Zoe asked. "A bunch of us are going to Backcountry."

I wasn't sure who the 'us' was or whether I was ready for the infamous Sunday nights. "I don't have a fake ID."

"I don't either. They don't care up here. They just want the business."

"Really?"

"Yeah."

I was toweling off Logan's legs. Mike had left me terrified of Logan's getting rain rot. Thanks to Mike, though, bathing Logan was going much better, as evidenced by the fact that only Logan was wet and I was still dry. "Okay, I guess."

"You could use to go out."

"You saw my round today?"

"Round?" Zoe said.

"Okay, my three jumps." I hesitated and then added, "This is really weird, but I think I saw that guy—Chris Kern—watching me today. And he was at the ring before too."

Zoe shrugged. "I don't know what's up with that. He did just break up with his girlfriend but, no offense, I don't really see you as his type."

I tried hard, but couldn't hide my curiosity. "Of course not, I mean, well, who was his girlfriend?"

Zoe explained that Chris had been dating another grand prix rider, Mary Beth McCord. They had been juniors together—the horse show equivalent of high school sweethearts. "He walked in on her with John Burke. Thank God she's off on tour in Europe now. Maybe he's on the prowl . . . checking out chicks in the jumper ring. The high A/Os were going after you—he might have his eye on some rich ammy. Look at Kevin Prince. He's totally got it made with the horses his wife's money buys him."

"Speaking of guys," I said. "Mike's really nice."

"Mike?" Zoe made a face. "Never in a million years is that happening."

"Really? But he's so nice and he clearly likes you."

Zoe shook her head. "The guy I'm totally after? He's Irish. I mean, *from* Ireland. Dermott Nugent. He's a jumper rider. Just that name, Dermott. Totally sexy. And his accent?"

I had finished with Logan's legs and stood up. "Is he a junior?"

"Junior, no! I don't date boys my age. You know that, right?"

I threw the towel in my dirty laundry pile. "I guess I forgot."

"He's maybe thirty."

"Thirty?"

"Well, I'm not sure exactly. But something like that. You have to see him." Zoe exhaled dramatically. "You'll see him tonight if you come out with us. You have to come."

I glanced around my tack stall. I still had to clean my tack and get Logan all put away. It was going to be a while. After only a few days of taking care of my own horse, I had new respect for grooms like Mike. Day after day they were at the barn before the sun was up and they were always the last ones to leave. They took care of four or five horses, not just one. I was physically exhausted from mucking Logan's stall and dragging the hose in and everything else I had to do that I never had even thought about before. But maybe I could leave some tack undone or not pick out Logan's stall . . .

"What time are you going?" I asked.

"Not till later, like eight or nine."

"Well, I guess that gives me plenty of time."

"To get ready?" Zoe looked at me like she was confused. I'm sure she'd noticed that I didn't exactly spend hours choosing an outfit or blowing out my hair.

I picked up my tack bucket, which I'd need to go fill with water. "No, to clean my tack and get everything put away."

"Oh." Zoe looked around. "So this is where being the good friend I am, I offer to help you, right?"

"That would be super amazing."

Zoe sighed. "I'm not really loving this you-doing-all-your-own-work thing."

I handed Zoe the bucket. "Ah, neither am I. Can you go ask Mike for some leather conditioner? I left mine open and I came back and found some dog licking the last bit of it up. I haven't gotten around to getting more yet."

Zoe's flirty smile immediately took over her face. "That I can totally do."

* * *

With Zoe's help, it only took an hour and a half to get everything done at the barn. If it had been just me, it would have taken at least three hours. As much as Zoe pretended to be one of the wealthy kids who'd never lifted a pitchfork, she actually knew a lot about horses. Usually I wouldn't have cared to learn any tricks of the trade, but I'd figured out that not knowing what I was doing made things take a lot longer. I was eager to learn any shortcuts. Zoe showed me how to pick out Logan's stall, quickly assessing where his pee spots were. "He probably goes in the same place all the time. Horses are like that—they choose a spot." She told me that if I could pick out the manure a few times throughout the day, cleaning his stall the next morning wouldn't be as involved. She also told me to come back to check on Logan each night. I could pick out his stall again and if it was chilly as it sometimes got on summer nights in Vermont, I could throw a light sheet on him. "That'll keep him warm and also keep him clean if he lies down, which equals less time spent getting out manure stains," she explained. Genius!

It was almost six by the time we left the barn. I was going to pick Zoe up at her condo at eight. Jed's parents had come in for the weekend and were taking him out to the fancy, expensive French bistro. Zoe said he was going to try to come by later if he could escape them.

Cheryl was sitting on the couch when I came into the condo. Her little Jack Russell, Maven, was on her lap and she had a trashy magazine in her hands. Cheryl showed in the younger A/O hunters and jumpers, which made her somewhere over eighteen and younger than thirty-five. She didn't seem to work. Instead, she spent her days following the show circuit from New England and New York in the summers to Florida in the winters. She had three horses, lots of designer handbags, and dated a guy who was a course designer. My mother had made my father promise to have me live with someone who would be "mature and responsible." I guess the best they could come up with was Cheryl.

"You look ragged," she said as I came in carrying my ring bag and my wrinkled show jacket on a hanger.

"Long day."

Cheryl flipped a page of her magazine. "Did you show?"

"Uh, sort of."

"What does that mean?"

"I didn't make it around."

"Oh." Cheryl scrunched up her nose. She had a short bob of blonde hair and perfectly manicured nails that I didn't understand how anyone could ride with. "Sorry to hear it."

I shrugged. "I'm going to go shower. I'm going out tonight . . ." I paused, waiting to see if she'd express any protective-like behavior. "To Backcountry, I guess it's called."

"Cool," she said. "I'll probably see you there."

So much for "mature and responsible." I dumped my ring bag in my room. The condo was typical rental-bland: sturdy but plain furniture, the occasional throw rug, and a few landscape paintings on the walls. My room had two twin beds. I slept in one and kept all my clothes that didn't fit in the one dresser neatly organized on the other.

After a long, hot shower, I lay down on my bed. It was only six-thirty and I wasn't picking Zoe up till eight. I'd rest a few minutes and then get up, get something to eat, and figure out what I was going to wear.

Only, of course I fell dead asleep and woke when I heard Cheryl shut the front door. I checked the clock. Ten of eight.

Crap! I jumped up and riffled through clothes in my dresser. I wasn't sure what I should wear to a bar. Would I see Chris? I decided on jeans and a kind of tight white T-shirt. I ran into the bathroom to brush my hair. It had dried funny from being slept on and the best I could do was tie it up on the top of my head in a messy knot. Make-up? I didn't do much make-up, but this night did seem to call for a quick patting of pressed-powder and a little lipstick.

I dug around the bottom of the closet to find my ballet flats. When I got to Zoe's, she was sitting on her couch, drinking a glass of red wine. She looked even prettier than she did in her riding clothes. Her blond hair fell artfully over her shoulders, somehow both styled and natural at the same time. Mascara and eyeliner made her brown eyes stand out from her tan skin. She had on a sexy, shimmery tank top that slipped off her shoulders and kept showing her bra straps, with white jeans. Cute leopard print kitten heels completed the outfit.

"You look really good," I said.

She grinned. "Thank you. I hope Irish feels the same way."

# Chapter 8

ZOE WAS RIGHT. In Weathersville, Vermont, they really didn't care whether you had an ID. Still, I held my breath all the way through the entrance and tried to smile as over-21 as possible whenever I saw someone who looked like he might be an employee.

Backcountry had a small dance floor, a few pub tables, plus a pool table, darts, and basketball-shooting games. The seats at the bar and the pub tables were practically full.

"Look, there's Amanda," I said, spotting another student of Jamie's over by the darts.

"And there's Chris," Zoe said, looking toward the bar.

I immediately turned red. I was even more embarrassed that I was embarrassed because there was nothing between us at all. I was just some bad rider who had crashed into him in the ring. Like Zoe had said, I wasn't even his type.

"You want to meet him?"

"Um—"

"Come on, you did crash into him and everything."

Before I could come up with a reason we shouldn't, Zoe had pulled me toward the bar. Chris was drinking a beer, facing away from the bar so he could look out at the rest of the room. He was leaning back on the bar, slouching in the most sexy way I'd ever seen. I took a few moments to absorb what he looked like without his helmet on. Sometimes guys can look sort of cute with a helmet on but when you see them without it's a huge disappointment—bad hair or a weird forehead or something. But Chris without his helmet did not disappoint. Chris wasn't just horse-show-hot, he was real world hot. He was Hollywood hot. He had brown hair that was cut pretty short and his features were perfectly proportioned. I always felt like guys had one thing on their face that was wrong—a crooked nose, overly-thick eyebrows, a pointy chin, thin lips, goofy ears. Maybe it was just my way of finding fault with every guy I saw—as if they'd ever be interested in me anyway—but Chris's mouth, nose, lips, chin, and forehead were all perfect. It was really wrong that anyone should be so gorgeous.

I gave Zoe a last minute plea. It wasn't too late to flee to the other side of the bar. "I don't know. This feels weird—"

"We'll just get a drink next to him. What's the big deal?"

"Fine, but don't say I was the one who crashed into him or anything, okay?"

There was only one stool open, one down from Chris.

"We can share it," Zoe said.

"That's okay, I'll stand."

In fact, I preferred to stand. I was close to five-foot-seven now and maybe still growing a little, so standing next to Zoe as she sat on the bar stool made us pretty much at eye level. I had a great build for a rider—there were talented juniors who would have killed to have my height and slim frame. Of course, I had the body, but none of the talent.

Waiting for Zoe to say something to Chris, I had the sudden urge to start biting my nails, a habit I had supposedly abandoned years before. Now I had a trick that no one knew about. I would let my nails grow long and then alone, before bed, I would chew them down, leaving just enough white to still file and make it look like I had filed them to begin with. It was such a relief to chew them, even if it was only once a month. Afterwards, I always felt like I had the best night's sleep in forever.

But I swore to myself I would never chew them again in public. And now, as I wondered whether Chris would recognize me, was no time to break down.

Zoe ordered two rum-and-cokes and handed me one. I envied how automatic and mature the words rum-and-coke sounded coming out of her mouth.

The person between Zoe and Chris left and Zoe leaned forward on her stool. "Hey, Chris."

He turned to us. "Oh, hey, Zoe. What's up?"

His voice sounded different than when he had said, *watch where you're going next time.* More casual and calm.

"Not much," Zoe said. "How'd you do in the grand prix yesterday?"

"I was third with Titan."

"That's great. I was sorry to hear about Nova."

Chris hung his head a little. "Yeah, thanks."

"Wait, isn't Sunday when the grand prix goes?" I asked.

"Here they're on Saturdays because of HITS. Some of the riders keep horses here and at HITS so they can ride in the grand prix here on Saturdays and there on Sundays," Chris explained.

"Oh," I said, feeling like I should have known and certainly should have kept quiet.

Zoe said, "Chris, this is Hannah. She's up here for the summer. She rides with Jamie too."

"My condolences," Chris said. "I mean, on the riding-with-Jamie part."

I hadn't realized that other people knew how Jamie could be and it was such a relief. I laughed. "No kidding."

I waited for Chris to have some kind of revelation from looking at me. But he turned his head when a very tan man at the pool table said, "You wanted next game, right?"

Chris nodded and stood up, taking the cue from the guy's hand. He turned to me. "It was nice meeting you."

Zoe swiveled around in her seat. She held out her drink for me to clink glasses. "Now was that so bad?"

I clinked back. "I don't think he remembered me, thank God."

"To a great summer," Zoe said.

"To a great summer."

We both took a sip of our drinks. Half of Zoe's was already gone. I hadn't touched mine yet. It burned my throat. I must have made a face because Zoe laughed. "You're going to have to get into the swing of things. Sometime we're gonna have to come and get you totally plastered."

"Not tonight. I have to get up early and take care of Logan tomorrow."

"You didn't ask one of the guys to feed him?"

"No, should I have?"

Zoe shrugged. "If you want to sleep in on a Monday." Zoe looked down the bar. "Okay, we have to find Irish. I heard he'd be here tonight."

# Chapter 9

BY MIDNIGHT, ZOE HAD DOWNED two more rum-and-cokes and was dancing incredibly closely, even to fast songs, with Dermott. Dermott was cute, I did have to give Zoe that. And his accent was cool too. But there was something I didn't really like about him. He was loud and boisterous and funny and kind of too much of all those things.

Jed had never shown up. Maybe he had texted Zoe but she wasn't exactly checking her phone. I had spent the night watching Chris and I was pretty sure I was completely in love with him. He seemed so confident, the total opposite of me, of course. He talked to people when he wanted to, roamed around the bar, just doing whatever he felt like and he didn't seem to be worrying about what he looked like or what people thought of him. He also did this thing that I loved. When he was talking to someone and they said something funny he kind of tossed his head back quickly. Whenever he did that, I felt it in my stomach. And maybe somewhere else too.

I was against the wall opposite the bar thinking of how pathetic I must look, standing alone, when Chris, who according to my count had drunk three beers, won two games of pool and lost one, and had talked to two girls, walked by. He went in the bathroom and passed me again on his way back. This time, he slowed down, glanced at me and then stopped.

"Hannah, right?"

I nodded. "Hi."

Chris wagged his finger at me. "I swear I know you from somewhere."

My back stiffened against the wall behind me.

"Wait a second. You're the one... you crashed into me on warm-up day, didn't you?"

I tried to smile, hoping we could laugh it off. It could become one of those funny remember-when moments.

He did the thing where he tossed his head back and I felt my knees weaken.

"It was you, wasn't it? I didn't recognize you without your helmet."

"I'm so sorry," I said.

Chris leaned toward me and I could smell the beer on his breath. It smelled sweet and earthy, almost like when you press your nose to a flake of hay, which I hadn't ever done until a few days ago. I hadn't really smelled beer breath before, either. So many new things. "Do you always go crashing into people like that?"

"Not regularly, no."

"What happened? Forget your left from your right?"

"It's my horse, he's kind of psycho."

"There you go, blame your horse. Oldest trick in the book."

"No, seriously, he is."

"There's no such thing as a crazy horse only a crazy person for buying him."

"Well, I didn't buy him. I got him as a present so does that still make me crazy?"

"No, I guess it makes the person who gave him to you crazy."

I laughed. "That sounds about right. It was my dad."

"Where'd he get him from? Didn't Jamie pick him out?"

I shook my head. "It's kind of a long story, but he bought him sight unseen. Kind of on a whim, I guess you'd say." I paused and then added, "Seventeenth-birthday-guilt gift."

Chris stepped back. "You're seventeen?"

"No, I'm eighteen. But I got him when I was seventeen."

This seemed to make Chris relax although I didn't know why he cared about my age. It was hard to believe he'd consider liking me and, even if he did, I had learned from Zoe that most of the horse show guys didn't care how young the girls were they messed around with. She'd once told me her first time was when she was fourteen with T.J. Jones, a grand prix rider who was at least ten years older than she was. Chris was only twenty-three. But maybe Chris was different from other over-sexed morally-bankrupt riders. It seemed like the lopsided ratio of women to men boosted horse show guys' testosterone, turning many into instant womanizers. Could Chris be different and actually have a conscience?

"What was he feeling guilty about?" Chris asked.

"Not being around much. My parents divorced when I was pretty young and except for vacations and a few weeks in the summer I've spent most of my time with my mom."

I started to worry that I was saying too much. I didn't even know this guy and I was telling him my life story?

"My parents are divorced too. It sucks, doesn't it?"

"Definitely." I was surprised to hear him say it sucked. Somehow I thought when you got older it didn't suck as much.

"I envy people who have parents that are happily married, or amicably divorced, at least. My parents can't come to the same horse show. When I rode in the World Cup Final they took turns coming on alternate days. I mean we're in Sweden and it's the World Cup and you can't even be in a stadium with thousands of people together? No one says you have to sit together, or even see each other. My brother was the only one from my family that could be there each day. I can't imagine what they'll do if I make the Olympics."

That was the first time I'd ever heard anyone talk seriously, yet casually, about making the Olympics. It was pretty cool.

"Does your brother ride too?"

"Nope. I'm the only one in the family who rides. How about you?"

"Yeah, same, just me."

"What about your parents?" Chris asked. "Do they get along?"

I held my hand up in the universal sign for so-so. "They

live on separate coasts so they don't have to see each other much, but they usually pull it together for big events like graduations or birthdays. How did you do at the World Cup, anyway?" I felt like I should know—most people at the show probably did.

"Good. I was fifth."

"Zoe said something about a horse you had that was hurt?" Again, I felt dumb for not knowing what was probably common knowledge, but Chris didn't seem annoyed.

"Yeah, my World Cup horse, actually. He got hurt at Devon. That's why I didn't go on the Tour this summer and that's why I came here instead of going to Spruce." He hesitated like he understood I might not even know what the Tour or Spruce was. After all, I hadn't known about the grand prix being on Saturday. I did actually know about the tours to Europe arranged by the United States Equestrian Team and I knew about Spruce Meadows in Canada. Chris continued, "This is a nice circuit for young grand prix horses. Jumps aren't huge, courses are nice. Hey, did you drive here?"

"Yeah."

"Would you give me a ride home?"

"Okay, I'm just not sure when I'm leaving. I mean I drove Zoe."

"Look—" I had briefly lost track of Zoe and he put one hand on my shoulder and pointed with the other to the corner of room by the darts where Zoe was intertwined with Dermott. "I don't think you need to worry about driving her home."

"I guess you're right." It was what Zoe had wanted—to

hook up with Dermott. But I kind of felt sad about the way it was happening. I kept thinking about her at age fourteen and whether that had set things up for her in a bad way.

"You didn't drive here?" I asked him.

"No. I wanted to get really drunk, but I didn't follow through with it, and now I just kind of want to get out of here. I'm ready to leave whenever you are."

I looked over the clusters of people. "I still think I should tell Zoe I'm leaving. Just in case she wants to go home."

"Okay." Chris removed his hand. I wanted it back. I really wanted it back.

I made my way across the room to Zoe. Dermott had his hands on her butt and I tried to look blasé about it as I tapped Zoe on the shoulder.

She barely pulled away. "Zoe, sorry but I was thinking of leaving. Do you need a ride?"

Zoe looked at Dermott, kissed him once more and then said, "Nah, sweetie, go ahead."

"Okay, actually Chris asked me to give him a ride home, can you believe that?"

Zoe made suggestive eyes at me. "Don't do anything I wouldn't do!"

I turned to head across the room to Chris. *Don't do anything I wouldn't do?* Chris just wanted a ride home, right? I wasn't missing signals or something? He didn't actually want to hook up with me?

I told Chris we were all set to leave.

"What did I tell you," he said. "Luck of the Irish. These European guys . . ." Chris trailed off. I wondered if he was thinking about Mary Beth in Europe. Maybe that was why he wanted to get drunk?

The lot was packed with SUVs and trucks angled onto the grass in places. It was Sunday night, after all. Music was blaring from inside. The license plates were from all different states—Northeastern states, but also plates from as far away as Florida, South Carolina, and Kentucky.

When we were pulling out, I said, "Zoe, I guess she does that sort of thing a lot?"

"What sort of thing?" Chris said.

"Well, I don't know. I mean I kind of can't believe her, with Dermott."

"Oh, that." Chris shrugged. "I don't exactly keep track. A lot of wild stuff happens up here."

My high school had been exactly the same, with people getting drunk at parties and hooking up. But I stayed away from that crowd. I hadn't been to one party, not even the annual graduation party at the beach that I promised myself I'd go to. Ryan, my older brother, had been one of the most popular kids in our high school. I'd never been able to keep up with his popularity so I'd stopped trying, instead falling into the role of the studious sibling. Before he left for college, Ryan always invited me to hang out with his friends. He was nice that way—always trying to include me. One time I'd messed around with one of his friends. He went up my shirt and down my pants and that was okay, if not extremely pleasurable, but when he undid his own zipper and started to pull himself out, I'd gotten nervous and shut him down. That was the extent of my sexual history. Sometimes I regretted stopping him. Maybe it would have been better to have gone all the way with him, even if it didn't exactly feel right or like I imagined it would be. After Ryan graduated and wasn't there to include me in things, it was easy enough to slip into the background. I had a few friends, but like me, they cared more about their grades than partying and hooking up.

Now, I wondered, did Chris want to have sex with me? If he wanted to, would I? I was certainly really attracted to him. Could I be like Zoe and just go for it? Is that why Chris had wanted to get really drunk—to screw someone and forget all about his ex, Mary Beth? Had she found someone else in Europe?

"So you're up here for the whole circuit?" Chris asked.

"Yup, it's going to be a long one judging from week one."

"You mean what your horse does in the ring, or the way Jamie yells at you?"

I glanced quickly at Chris and then looked back at the road. "Where are you staying?"

"Off Route 12. Know where it is?"

I nodded. I was off Route 12 too.

"So you don't want to talk about it now, your horse being a total shit like that?" Chris said.

"No, I just can't believe you noticed."

"I happened to be standing nearby."

I pulled onto Route 12 and started winding up the mountain. We passed signs for ski parking and deer crossing.

"Next right," Chris said. "The first house on the left."

I pulled onto the road and then into the driveway and put the car in park. His house was an A-frame ski-lodge type made of dark timbers. "So you knew who I was? I mean, when Zoe and I came up to you at the bar? Did you know that was me?"

"Yeah."

"Oh," I said, still unsure what it all meant.

"You pretended you didn't know who I was too," Chris pointed out.

"I was mortified."

Chris tossed his head back, not fully but just a little. I couldn't figure out where this was going. Was he going to ask me to come in? Or did he actually like me, and want more than just sex?

"I'll help you with him if you want," Chris said.

"What?"

"I'll help you with your psycho horse."

Out of all the things to come out of Chris's mouth this was the one I least expected. "Why would you want to do that?"

"I don't know. I just will."

"But how? What about Jamie?" None of this made any sense. My head was spinning. Grand prix riders didn't just randomly offer to help riders who already had a trainer, especially not ones as accomplished as Chris Kern.

"Tomorrow morning. Six o'clock, in the hunter warm-up. It's Monday—she won't find out."

"Really?" Here I had been weighing whether I'd have sex with him and all he was offering was to give me a lesson. I didn't know what to think.

Chris got out of the car. He leaned back in and said, "Get some sleep and I'll see you bright and early."

The whole world seemed hooded and eerily quiet as I drove back onto Route 12, up the mountain a minute more, and to my condo. None of what had just happened seemed real.

Still, I got into bed and set my alarm for 4:45. It was only a few short hours away, but I knew I wouldn't have any trouble getting up when the alarm went off.

As I fell asleep I thought about Zoe and Dermott. I imagined myself in the bar like Zoe had been only it wasn't Dermott who had his hands all over me. It was Chris.

# Chapter 10

IT WAS STILL DARK when I led Logan from his stall. I used the stepladder to mount and walked across the desolate show grounds to the back ring. The sun was just edging out from behind the mountains that surrounded the grounds, casting a dim light over everything. I could see Logan's breath coming out of his nostrils.

Logan hadn't even had time to eat and I hadn't either. The only person who was in the tent when I'd gotten there was the nearly sleepwalking horse watch guy doing his last check of the night. The whole time as I was driving to the show and getting Logan tacked up, I was wondering if Chris would show up, or if he'd only been messing with me.

And why should he show up? A top rider with his sights set on the Olympics stopping to help some nobody and her psycho horse? Get up early on his one off-day? It couldn't be a way to get into my pants—he hadn't even tried to kiss me the night before—and I knew nearly every girl at the show would want to sleep with Chris Kern.

I entered the schooling ring. There was no sign of Chris. I would have to slink back to the barn after all. I looked at my watch—I would give him five minutes, ten at the most. I heard footsteps behind me. I turned quickly in the saddle to see Chris with a travel coffee mug in his hand.

I guess my face looked surprised because he said, "Didn't think I would come, huh?"

"I wasn't sure."

Chris looked at his watch. "Sorry, I'm late. Let's get to work. Make a circle around me and get to the posting trot. Let me see this horse go."

I straightened my back at Chris's words. He was all business, making the guy I'd talked to last night about divorce feel like a dream. Maybe he'd been more drunk than I'd realized.

I squeezed Logan into a trot and started a large circle around him. Chris took a sip from his mug and then said, "Make your circle smaller."

I brought in my circle. I trotted four revolutions around Chris before he said, "Now, change your direction and trot the other way."

I reversed direction, keeping my head straight and my eyes focused in front of me. Every once in a while, though, I would glance over at Chris, hoping to see him without being seen. But Chris was staring straight back at me, watching Logan the whole time, studying us.

Finally he said, "Now, let me see you canter."

After I had cantered in both directions, Chris motioned to me. "Okay, bring him down to a walk and come here for a second." His voice turned thoughtful. "What this horse needs is consistency. His trot is erratic, always changing pace. Same with his canter. His frame is all over the place. No wonder when you get in the ring or try to jump he's out of control. He's at loose ends, all the time."

I nodded.

"What kind of flatwork do you do with Jamie?"

I shrugged. "Not much, just hacking mostly."

Chris shook his head. "Well, let's get to it. Get back on the circle, posting trot."

I returned to the circle and picked up a posting trot, my heartbeat quickening to match Logan's racing stride.

"Okay," Chris said. "We're going to start right there. Shorten up your reins about two inches so there's no slack."

I shortened my reins and could immediately feel Logan's neck muscles stiffen as he began mouthing the bit.

"That's fine for him to tense up like that. Now apply both leg and some pressure on the reins. This horse needs both leg and hand together to make him come together."

"That's what he doesn't like."

Chris chuckled. "Well, that's too bad. He doesn't like going over the jumps either but are you going to let him keep stopping on you?"

I shook my head and concentrated on applying both leg and hand at the same time.

"Always leg first and always more leg than hand," Chris added.

Logan threw his head up in the air and tried to race forward.

"Don't worry about that." Chris took a sip of his coffee.

"He's trying to evade you there—to find a way out of having to work."

The sun was further up in the sky, casting a pretty glow on the show grounds. A few more trucks had pulled up to the tents, grooms reporting to work while all the trainers and riders slept.

"It's going to take time. But once we teach him the right aids, he'll understand what you're asking. Keep squeezing him forward like you're doing, but instead of just pulling steadily on the reins, half-halt him."

I looked at Chris. "I don't think I know what..."

Chris let out a disgusted sigh, but I could tell his disappointment was at Jamie, not me. "A half-halt is when you take firmly on the reins and then release. You can half-halt every other stride if you need to. If you hang on the reins it's just going to get him more upset and it won't teach him anything."

I tried what he said. Why hadn't Jamie bothered to teach me any of this? She had once been a good horsewoman and she still had a reputation for turning out winners, even though it was fading as new trainers came onto the scene. But why hadn't Jamie tried harder with me? Was it because my dad went solo and bought a crazy horse, cheating her out of a hefty commission? Was it because I was clearly a bad rider, beyond help? Had she treated me better when I leased Dobby?

"Let's see you keep trotting, applying your leg against his side and using half-halts at various points around the circle when you feel him speed up."

I pressed my leg against Logan's side. Immediately he started to speed up again. I took once on the reins and then softened my hand like Chris said to.

"Good," Chris said. "Keep doing that until you get the hang of it. A rider's tendency is to use the reins for balance and therefore we feel uncomfortable letting go of the horse's mouth. It'll get easier as you get stronger and more in tune with him. Keep going."

Even though his words were far from incredible praise, they were positive and they washed over me warmly. I don't think I'd ever heard Jamie say something to me as positive as "good."

I trotted more revolutions around Chris, working on pushing Logan from my leg into my hand.

"More leg," Chris said. "I know it feels backwards, but you need more leg, not more hand. There—" Logan started to soften through his neck and come down onto the bit. "Feel that?"

"Yes!" I did feel it and it was magical for a moment. Logan was becoming more supple to my aids. But then that feeling was gone again and Logan was racing forward, his head high.

"You'll have him for a few strides and then lose it. That's the way it happens—slowly. When you get it, don't completely throw the reins away at him. You never want a slack in the reins. You want to keep a constant feel, a constant connection to his mouth and that connection can vary slightly from half-halt to giving back, but no slack or constant pulling. Good. There he's listening and you can soften to him a little. Just like that. That's his reward for doing what you ask. Excellent. There you have him again. You'll get him for a few strides and then lose him again, he'll quicken and then it's push him to your hand and half-halt again and give back and all over again."

Between listening to Chris's voice and feeling the first moments of progress I'd ever felt with Logan, I was actually enjoying my ride, which was something I hadn't felt since I'd ridden Dobby. This was why I liked riding—I thought to myself—I remembered this!

"Let's go ahead and canter."

I picked up the left lead canter and immediately Logan surged forward.

"It's the same thing at the canter, only harder. Don't just pull against him on the reins at the canter—that will only make him go faster. Take and give. Don't forget to use your leg."

I sat deep into the back of the saddle using my leg to push Logan toward my hand. But Chris told me I was driving him more and to lighten my seat and try to sit only on the front of my seat bones. Logan began to slow down and I relaxed as the circle began to take longer and longer to complete.

"That's right," Chris said. "He likes to get mad and do whatever he pleases, but now you've got him between your leg and your hands, which is correct. Now he's listening. Good. Just like that. Just like that! Excellent and let him walk."

Instead of coming back to the walk right away Logan rambled on from the canter to the trot and then finally to the walk.

"We have to get your transitions sharper too," Chris said. "He needs to be listening to you in everything he does."

I nodded and reached down to pat Logan. After a brief rest, we changed directions and worked on the canter again. It was Logan's easier direction and for a few more moments I felt him round his neck and back and collect underneath me. My transition back to the walk was still weak, though.

Chris looked at his phone. "We better call it quits for today."

"We're not going to jump him?" I was actually exhausted from all the flatwork, but with Jamie we never just flatted. So this was it, one lesson with Chris and it was going to be all on the flat?

"Not today."

"But that's the worst part. That's where I need the most help."

"We'll get to it," Chris said.

I smiled. So this wasn't my one and only lesson with Chris. For whatever bizarre reason, he was interested in teaching me again. And for the first time in forever, I felt I'd actually learned something from a lesson.

"Thanks," I said.

Chris nodded. "Tomorrow, same time."

"Great. That would be great. Um, what do I owe you?"

"Nothing," he said.

"Really?"

"Yes, I'm certain about that."

I looked out over the empty show grounds. The jump standards were grouped in the middle of the rings with the rails leaning against them. Mondays were strange, like everyone had disappeared overnight.

"Chris?"

"Yeah?"

"What about Jamie? What if someone saw me and tells her I was out riding?"

"Say you thought he needed a good hack, that's all. She won't find out because no one else is going to know, okay? We'll do it super early and keep this between you and me."

"Right," I said.

Chris nodded. "We'll fix him. I promise."

I knew I should look away from Chris, but I couldn't and we were both kind of staring at each other. Finally, Chris said, "Well, see you later."

I walked back to the barn on a total high. The fact that I'd gotten no sleep, was tired from my lesson, and still had all my morning barn chores to do didn't matter in the slightest.

Zoe called me later that morning when I was sitting on my tack trunk having a protein bar. "Was I hallucinating or did you and Chris leave together?"

"Yeah, but it wasn't like that. I just drove him home."

"No kissing? No car-groping?"

"No, definitely not." I wanted to tell Zoe Chris was helping me, but he had said we should keep it a secret. Zoe didn't exactly seem like the type who could keep a secret.

"How was . . . well, you know, with Dermott?"

"Amazing. I really think this could be something, you know? He was super sweet when we said good-bye this morning." Zoe gave an audible yawn. "Okay, I'm going back to sleep. I just had to check in with you. I didn't think anything happened with Chris, but I had to check. I mean, you and Chris Kern? No way."

So there it was—no way.

Chris was helping me with Logan and I had to forget about it being anything more than that.

# Chapter 11

BUT FORGETTING ABOUT CHRIS wasn't so easy, especially when he was giving me a lesson every morning. I got used to seeing him and hearing his voice on a daily basis. I kept waiting for him to say the lessons were over, or just not show up one morning. But he was always there, coffee mug in hand. Six o'clock became my favorite hour of the day, and I looked forward to it with a fierce intensity I didn't know I was capable of. I lived for that hour with Chris.

I kept thinking we would start to jump, but all we did was flatwork. At the end of each lesson, we would generally stare at each other for a few prolonged moments and then one of us would awkwardly say something and we'd head off in our separate directions.

For the rest of each day, I kept tabs on where Chris was as much as was humanely possible between my own riding and taking care of Logan. What Zoe had taught me about picking out Logan's stall was definitely helpful and whether I liked it or not, I was getting better at mucking out too. I developed a little routine. First pick out any big piles of manure. Then bank clean shavings, get the heavy pee-soaked shavings, and any errant manure balls that rolled down the banks. More banking, since I became obsessive about getting out every last piece of manure. Then bring the banks down somewhat, add however much new bedding was needed, and spread it all out neatly. I never thought I would admit it, but there was a weird satisfaction in finishing Logan's stall and having it all clean and perfect for him.

Logan kept pooping in his water buckets. Not every day, but a few times a week. I swear on those days he came right over to greet me when I got there in the morning like he was saying, "Hello, look what I have in store for you today!" It seemed like it was his own little way of saying FU to me. I laughed about it with Mike. Instead of making me madder at Logan, in a weird way I almost respected him for it. The not-so-little bugger had a mind of his own. It became our own personal inside joke—if you can have an inside joke with a horse. I'd arrive in the morning, see the poop, and say, "Poop in the water bucket again, Logan? Can't you be a little more creative? It's getting very stale. You gotta up your game, bud."

When I had gotten Logan put away, fed him his morning grain, scrubbed the water buckets with bleach-water as Mike had shown me to do when the pooping became a recurring thing, and refilled them, I was usually pretty beat. But I still managed to go up to the food truck and get a bagel. I'd linger around the jumper rings, trying to be inconspicuous while I scoped out where Chris might be that particular day. He had his two grand prix horses and a few young horses that he showed in the 1.30 meter classes. He didn't have any customers, though, so he was mostly showing in the grand prix ring. From the spectator tent or bleachers I could watch him walk the course, warm up, and show without him noticing me. Or so I thought.

It was clear from watching him that he was well liked. In the course walk, riders were always talking to him and even the course designer stopped to chat with him. When he schooled his horses, his barn manager, Dale, set his jumps. I couldn't imagine not having a trainer, but Chris seemed able to do it all himself. In the ring, he rode flawlessly, in sync with his horses. Some jumper riders had unorthodox styles— rounded backs, legs swinging back in the air, or toes down in the stirrups. These were things I'd never really noticed before but then again I'd never spent much time watching before. I arrived for my lessons, rode, and went home. And when I showed I came for my classes and then left. Now that I was at the show more, I was seeing a whole new world I'd missed.

Chris, on the other hand, had impeccable equitation. Some riders rushed around, pulling and pumping. Maybe they ended up with clean rides, but they never looked good doing it. Every round Chris rode looked smooth and effortless. His horses seemed to love him. They trusted him and wanted to do their best for him. With the young horses he seemed to take his time and not rush a horse in the jump-off.

In between classes, he spent time either back at his barn, which was two tents away from Jamie's, or hanging out around the rings. Often he'd be on his phone and I'd wonder whom he was talking to, and a few times I saw him talking to a girl who rode in the amateur-owner jumpers.

The rest of the hours of the day I stalked Chris in my mind, imagining everything he was doing and often imagining interactions we might have, should we bump into each other at the food truck, tack store, or in-gate.

Meanwhile, Zoe was doing some actual stalking of Dermott, trying to figure out what was going on between them. He was nice enough to her when he saw her, but there was nothing more than that and Zoe said it was like they hadn't ever slept together. On Thursday, I went with her to watch the $10,000 Welcome Class. She thought I was going solely to support her, but I had the ulterior motive that Chris was showing in the class too.

Dermott had two to ride and Chris one. Dermott wasn't one of the top Irish riders. He wasn't a fixture on the Irish team, but maybe someday he'd be. He'd jumped over the pond for the summer with a bunch of horses to sell. His father owned a breeding yard outside of Dublin and they knew they could get a bunch of horses sold if Dermott showed them and people got to watch them and try them. He'd also brought a good grand prix horse that wasn't for sale—unless someone offered an obscene price. That horse, Gendarme, was his shot for the next Olympics. All this information Zoe told me as we watched Dermott walk the course. She'd gleaned some of it from talking to Dermott, some from asking around, and some from the osmosis of hanging around the jumper in-gates.

There was a general air of cockiness and swagger about Dermott that I didn't like. I'd noticed it at the bar and it was even more evident at the show. But, if anything, his attitude seemed to draw Zoe to him. After the course walk, Dermott and Chris warmed up. Dermott ordered his ground crew around, barking at them to "raise this" or "change that." He could ride—there was no doubt about that. But he wasn't exactly a picture of beauty. I noticed how he posted high in the saddle at the trot, and sat behind the motion at the canter. His back was rounded and when he rode to a distance his elbows poked out. With his first horse, he had a rub that managed to stay up and after he exited the ring he was joking loudly with Nate McLean.

"You got so lucky, man," Nate said.

Dermott grinned. "I *always* get lucky."

Chris was the opposite of Dermott. Everything he did was controlled, meticulous, and quietly serious. He was polite to Dale and to the in-gate guy. I tried not to stare too much at him, afraid Zoe would notice, although she was too busy staring at Dermott. She seemed to think his sexual jokes were funny, not offensive.

"He says if he sells all his horses his father might ship another batch and he'll stay through the fall. He said he likes it here." Chris came into the ring and Zoe added, "He's already sold one." Zoe looked at Chris and shook her head. "I still can't believe you crashed into him."

"It was so embarrassing. But he was really nice about it. Anyway, can we just forget about it by now?"

"He's a nice guy," Zoe said. "He deserves to find someone this summer."

Me, I thought. But I'd never say it.

"And we totally need to find a man for you."

Chris was clean halfway through the course. Every jump he rode, I felt a kind of spasm in my stomach, but I tried to hide any emotions from Zoe.

"I'm not really looking for a relationship."

"I'm not talking about a relationship. I'm talking about a circuit fling." Zoe looked wistful. "I remember my first circuit fling—T.J. Jones."

"Wasn't he like ten years older than you?

Zoe shrugged. "Yeah, so?"

I couldn't imagine what it was like to be her, traveling the show circuit at age fourteen, having sex with T.J. Jones. And I had thought Chris, at twenty-three, was too old for me! But Zoe didn't seem sad about it. If anything it seemed like good memories.

"T.J. was so sweet. The day after the first time we slept together he put roses on the windshield of my car. We actually stayed together a while after the summer, then it kind of fizzled." Zoe looked at me. "Who was your first?"

I swallowed and I must have looked embarrassed because she said, "Oh my God, really?"

I expected her to start giving me a hard time, but instead she said, "That's cool. I get it. Waiting for the right guy is worth it. I've been with some assholes and I'm glad T.J. was my first. I'll always look back and be happy about it. So we have to find you someone super sweet and nice. What kind of guys do you like? Older? Your age? Tall? Short?"

I snuck a look at Chris, who was clean going to the last jump. "I haven't really had many boyfriends."

"Seriously? Because you're super pretty. Guys probably like you, but think you're too smart for them or something."

I felt touched that Zoe thought I was pretty and smart, instead of just a hopeless dork.

"You could have a lot of guys," she added.

So far there was only one guy I wanted. Chris had jumped the last jump clean and was leaving the ring.

"We'll find you the right guy. You don't want to go to college a virgin. I think it's better to find someone nice this summer. This is my new mission." Zoe smiled. "This'll be fun."

"You're not going to, like, tell anyone?"

"What? No. Not even Jed, unless you say it's okay. He can be helpful—good gaydar. One summer I spent the whole circuit chasing after this guy and he turned out to be gay. I mean he didn't really know it yet, but Jed can tell even before guys know it themselves. He's got a serious skill."

"I guess it's okay if Jed knows. As long as you think he won't go telling other people."

"No way. He's the master at keeping secrets. Kids at his school don't even know he's gay."

"Seriously?"

"He's waiting till college to come out to the world, although his parents know."

I couldn't imagine keeping a secret that big. The toll it would take. There had been openly gay kids in my school, but the suburb I lived in was wealthy, educated, and probably more tolerant than the town Jed was from. "Where's he going to school?"

"NYU."

"That'll be a change."

"For the better. Where are you going again?"

"Tufts." I hesitated and then said, "You're not going to school?" I wasn't sure, but I'd heard rumors.

"No. I'm going to ride for a living anyway so what's the point. I'm not very good at school stuff."

Zoe scanned the in-gate. "I'm looking at everything with a whole new eye now. Looking for the right man for you."

I didn't know what Zoe was seeing, but my eye fell squarely on Chris.

# Chapter 12

ZOE, JED, AND I BECAME kind of a pack. I'd never been part of a pack before and it was as good as it had looked when I was the one on the outside watching the packs of friends hanging out together at school. We cheered each other on whenever possible. Jed and I watched Zoe a lot. She was such a good rider and she got asked to catch ride all the time, especially in the junior hunters. She was qualified for the equitation so she just did the Washington and the Talent Search. She was busy riding a lot of the time, but when she wasn't on a horse, she and I went to watch Jed. He had a nice large junior hunter and he did the eq too.

On Friday, Zoe had an unusual break from riding and came with me to watch Jed in the Medal. He was qualified for the Maclay, but had suffered a string of bad luck mishaps in the Medal and still needed a few points. Zoe took a water out from her ring bag and we sat on the sidelines. We stopped talking when he entered the ring. We had to be silent or else we'd jinx him—that had become our superstition when any of us were in the ring. Although the whole show could be silent and it wouldn't be enough to help me. I felt like Chris's daily lessons were helping me figure Logan out on the flat, but it hadn't really translated into my classes yet. I kept having stops, only sometimes getting around the whole course. When I did get over all the jumps I usually had at least one or two rails and lots of time faults. Jamie yelled at me some days and other days said very little. I had the feeling she wished I wasn't riding with her.

Jed looked like he was going to be tight to an oxer midway through what had been a super good trip and Zoe leaned back like she was trying to ride the jump herself and fit in the stride. Jed's horse covered up the tight distance pretty well and Jed finished the rest of the course perfectly. He had pretty good equitation. We had to wait until he had completely left the ring before we could talk. Zoe let out a gust of air, like she'd been holding her breath, not just being silent.

"Oh my God, I thought he was totally going to chip, but it didn't look bad," she said.

"The rest was really good."

"That always happens to Jed. One-jump Jed. That's what Jamie calls him, because he always has one bad jump. But don't say it to him—he hates being called that."

The rest of the rounds were pretty weak, since it was late in the season and most of the top riders were qualified. Zoe was confident Jed would get called back for the test. She could pin a class just by watching from the in-gate and most of the time she got it right.

"You also have to consider who's judging," Zoe said.

I looked across the ring to the judges' booth. Zoe knew all the judges and they knew her too. I didn't know why I was even looking—besides George Morris, I didn't know one single judge.

"Who is it?"

"Adam Evans."

"And he likes Jed?"

"He likes all teenage boys," Zoe said. "If you Google him, you'll find out he likes them a little *too much*."

"What?"

"Exposing himself to a class from a boys' school on a field trip . . ."

"Seriously?" Sometimes the horse show world blew my mind. "How can he still be judging?"

"He had a good lawyer," Zoe said.

There were still fifteen riders left to go so Jed came over to talk to us.

"I came around the corner to that oxer and saw nothing," Jed said.

"It didn't look bad," Zoe reassured him. "It worked out. You'll test."

Jed held up his crossed fingers. "I just want to get this over with so I can relax and enjoy the rest of the circuit."

We watched a few rounds before Jed went back to get on early for the test. The judge wouldn't announce the test till everyone had ridden, but Jamie would have Jed practice the common tests, like trotting a jump, in the schooling area. His number was added to the standby list and Zoe guessed that he was in second place going into the test. He needed to be first or second to be qualified, although third or fourth would get him a few more points too.

"I'm having one of my brilliant thoughts," Zoe said as we watched the few remaining riders.

"About Jed?"

"No, you. About the absolute perfect guy to guide you through your virginal deflowering."

I shuddered. "That makes it sounds awful, like a medical procedure."

"Sorry. It's not awful. I mean it's not amazing sex the first time, but it's not bad."

"Painful?" I was definitely curious, not that I believed it was going to happen this summer.

"A little. A few drinks can help with that."

"I think I want to be sober."

Zoe shrugged. "It's *your* virginity." She pointed subtly to the tent near the in-gate. "Nick. Used to be a gate guy. Now he's doing some announcing. Unattached, nice, cute. Perfect for the job."

I squinted to the tent where was sitting at a table on a folding chair. I couldn't really see him from where we were but no matter what he looked like I was sure he wouldn't compare to Chris. Losing my virginity before college did seem like a good idea, sort of like stocking up on essential items at Ikea so you didn't feel out of place or unprepared. But I wanted to lose it to Chris, not anyone else.

"This is good," Zoe said. "Come on."

She pulled me over to the tent where Nick was working. He wore a straw hat and was a little short, but technically he was cute. Yet, it didn't matter because all I cared about was Chris. One of the Hemsworth brothers could have been sitting under that tent and I'd still be uninterested.

"Nick, this is my friend, Hannah, she rides with Jamie too."

"Hey," Nick said, tipping his hat slightly up on his forehead.

The judge from the other hunter ring called in with results over Nick's walkie-talkie and he had to scribble them down. When he was done writing, he looked at me again and smiled. "I better announce these."

"Yeah, we just wanted to say a quick hi before we go watch the test," Zoe said. "Are you going out Sunday night?"

"Yeah." He glanced at me again, this time with more interest. "See you guys at Backcountry?"

"We'll be there," Zoe said.

We walked back to watch the test. "See?" Zoe said. "Perfect, right?"

The first rider entered the ring for the callback. The test was simple—what Zoe called a don't-lose-my-winner test. She said Adam didn't want to risk the riders making any huge mess-ups. She told me about a confusing medal test where all four riders went off course and the embarrassed judge had to re-test. This test had a trot jump, a few single fences, and asked riders to sit trot back to line.

Zoe kept half an eye on the ring. "Do you like Nick?"

"I just met him."

"Yeah, but could you imagine doing it with him? I meet a guy and I immediately put him in one of three categories: hell-yeah, maybe, or no way, not even stranded on a desert island."

I glanced at Jed, waiting in line for the test. "I guess 'maybe.'"

The rider went back to line and it was Jed's turn. His test was good except for the trot jump, which was a little weak. I guess the nickname one-jump Jed was right.

Zoe clapped for Jed. "'Maybe' is a good start."

# Chapter 13

MY MOM TEXTED AND CALLED me a lot more often than my dad. She called every other day to check in. Usually I'd just tell her everything was fine. She never called Logan by his name. She called him "the horse." As in, "How's the horse?"

My mom wasn't like other horse show moms, who really got into their kids' riding. She didn't like to sit and watch my lessons. She didn't like coming to the shows and she didn't want to live vicariously through me. She didn't constantly ask Jamie why I wasn't winning or how I could do better. I guess all those things would be not half bad, a welcome departure from some of the crazy horse show mothers, if the reason behind it wasn't that she suffered from serious anxiety. Like such bad anxiety that she spent most of her days at home, binoculars around her neck, filling her bird-feeders and keeping up with her bird-themed blog, Feathered Friends. She took a whole slew of anti-anxiety meds and even so, she had panic attacks at places like the grocery store or the mall.

"Are you having fun?" Mom asked, when she called in the middle of the day on Saturday.

I sat down on my tack trunk, wiping the sweat off my forehead. It was going to be a hot one today and doing Logan's stall in the airless tent had felt like twenty minutes on the elliptical.

"Definitely."

"Have you gotten any ribbons?"

"Um, no, but I've gotten around some courses."

My mom blew out a hostile breath. "That horse."

Logan often felt like a stand-in for Dad and Mom liked to direct her hostility toward him. It was hard because honestly I couldn't blame my dad for divorcing my mom. I mean who would want to be married to a woman who couldn't go out to dinner, or never wanted to go on trips? They had met in their early thirties, during one of Mom's good phases when she was working as the manager of a stationary store. My dad came in after his father's death, looking for help picking out cards for his mother to send to people who sent her condolence cards. My mom helped him out and I guess it was kind of a hard time for him and he fell for her. It was a whirlwind romance with her getting pregnant after three months of dating, them getting married, and then my brother coming along soon after. I often wondered how soon my dad realized my mom was wrong for him and he'd made a really bad mistake. Was it before I was born, or after? Was it after Ryan was born?

"Mom, relax, okay, because it gets better. There's this guy, well, not just any guy but this rider, this amazing grand prix rider, Chris Kern, he's practically the best rider at the show and he offered to help me with Logan." I stopped, making sure no one could hear me. What was I doing anyway? Why was I telling my mother? At least I hadn't said I was already having him help me. I'd made it sound like I was thinking about it and checking with her.

"I don't know about that," Mom said.

"Why not?"

"Well, what about Jamie, and the fact that I don't even know this Chris, and neither do you. Is this your father's idea?"

"No, he doesn't know anything about it."

Again, she went right after Dad. As much as I couldn't blame him for divorcing her, I guess I couldn't blame her for hating him. It wasn't fair that he got to live a normal, happy life and she was stuck figuring out ways to manage her anxiety, which often included way too many cocktails.

"He's like totally famous. Google him. You'll see." I had spent plenty of time myself reading everything I could find about Chris. He had a huge fan page on Facebook with the most gorgeous photographs of him competing at shows all over the world and lots of videos of him competing on YouTube. I learned that as a junior he'd won the Washington Equitation Finals, the USEF Talent Search, and had been second in the Medal Finals. The same year Mary Beth had won the Maclay Finals. I'd spent plenty of time reading about her too, something I wasn't very proud of. She was really pretty, with a gorgeous, huge smile and what looked like big boobs from what I could tell from the photos of her.

"Still, this worries me," Mom said.

What didn't worry her? Her whole life was spent worrying.

I detected silence on the other end. I checked my cell signal—sometimes it cut out in the mountains—but it was still at three bars. "Mom?"

"Sorry, I thought I saw a Kestrel in one of my nest-boxes, but it couldn't be."

I looked up at the ceiling of the tent and shook my head. My mom was obsessed with birds. It was the only thing that she found beyond drugs and booze that seemed to calm her. She had about ten bird feeders all over the yard, plus she grew specific plants and flowers that attracted particular birds. She had fountain birdbaths and birdhouses and roosting boxes. She was forever peering out windows and looking into binoculars. On her really good days, she went on bird walks at Audubon Sanctuaries and at the Mount Auburn Cemetery. She had a whole group of other "bird" friends online.

"But it wasn't. I saw one the other day, though. He flew in and sat on the oak and I swear it was like he was laughing at the world. Just sitting there laughing."

Usually I was desperate to get her to talk about anything besides birds, but right then I didn't mind so much since it meant she wasn't talking about Logan and what I'd said about Chris helping me.

"How's everything else? How's Cheryl? Is the condo working out?"

"It's great," I said, thinking of how Cheryl went to Back-country several nights a week, not just Sundays, came home late, and was still asleep when I left for the barn every morning. Nearly each morning I'd find a bottle of wine in the recycling bin.

"Good, good," Mom said.

We finished up our conversation. I told her everything would be fine and to go back to enjoying her birds. After we hung up, I stayed on the tack trunk and closed my eyes. I lay down, curling up in a fetal position. It wasn't comfortable but I was tired enough that I dozed off. Only horse people could sleep on a tack trunk. I woke up, hot and sticky, when Zoe and Jed pulled up in the golf cart and Zoe said, "Grand Prix time!"

Zoe waved for me to get in. "Come on—"

I hopped on next to Jed. Zoe stepped on the gas, jolting us forward. We parked by the ring. Zoe was walking slowly now, acting all casual as if moments earlier she hadn't been racing at top speed. The riders were walking the course. I located Chris right away. He had his hand on the back rail of an oxer with a liverpool underneath it, rolling the rail in the cups to see how easily it might come down.

Zoe whispered, "There he is. By the double."

Dermott was striding off the double combination.

The announcer's voice came over the P.A. "A few more minutes and we'll be set to go with our grand prix. Riders are finishing up their course walk."

Dermott looked back over the course one more time and then headed toward the in-gate.

"He goes late in the class," she told us. "I'm going to go talk to him."

Zoe shook out her hands like she was going on stage. I'd

never seen her nervous before. When it came to going into a big class, she had ice in her veins. But a guy she liked turned her inside out.

When she left, Jed said, "This is not good."

"Why not?"

"Because he totally doesn't like her."

"How do you know?" I wasn't sure if it was a guy thing, or if Jed had heard something.

"For one thing, it's obvious. But I've seen him flirting with about three other girls. He's a total *play-ah*." Jed exaggerated the word.

"Shouldn't we tell her?"

"Zoe isn't really good with people telling her things like that. When she was into Antonio and I told her he'd slept with Rachel, she didn't talk to me for a month. Talk about shooting the messenger."

Zoe was near the in-gate now. Dermott clearly saw her. She smiled at him and Jed and I held our collective breath. I didn't know which was worse—Dermott avoiding her, or talking to her and giving her false hope. He walked toward her and they started talking.

I was so engrossed in watching them that I hadn't noticed Chris had walked up to us. "What are you guys staring at?"

I whipped my head around. "Oh, um-"

Chris must have seen Zoe and Dermott. "Ah, I got you. What's going on with that?"

"Bad scene," I said.

"It's not pretty," Jed added.

Dermott was now walking away from Zoe. Instead of heading toward us, she took off in the opposite direction.

"Shit," Jed said. To Chris and me, he said, "I've got this one," and he jogged after her.

Chris raised his eyebrows. "I think anyone could have predicted how that would end."

"Do you know him?" I asked.

"Dermott? Not really. But I don't think you have to know him to know what's he about." Chris gazed out over the ring. The course was cleared and the jump crew was making a last minute adjustment to one of the timers.

"When do you go?" I asked.

"Fifteenth."

"So you should probably be watching."

"You can watch with me," he said.

The jump crew finished with the timer and the announcer said, "Looks like we're ready to go now with our $30,000 Grand Prix of the Mountains. This is a Table IIa class. For those of you in the stands that means our riders will jump our first course. They need to leave all the rails up and stay within the time-allowed. If they do that, they'll be invited back for the jump-off, a shortened course against the clock."

My phone rang and I looked at the screen. My dad. Of course. There was no doubt my mom had emailed him to complain about what I'd said about Chris wanting to help me. I pressed the button to silence the ringer.

"Who's that?"

"My dad."

"You're not answering it?"

"No. I'll call him back later."

"Was that really your dad? Sure it wasn't your boyfriend?"

I laughed. "I don't have a boyfriend." The idea that Chris would think I had a boyfriend was ridiculous.

"No?" He was watching the first rider on course, but it felt like he wanted to look at me.

"No, no boyfriend."

He nodded, a small smile on his face.

"Do you have a girlfriend?" I asked, feeling strangely bold.

"No. I'm unattached at the moment as well."

"At the moment?"

Now he looked at me. It was a crazy feeling looking into his eyes.

"I was dating someone for a while. But we broke up."

"I'm sorry," I said, even though I wasn't the least bit sorry.

Chris shrugged. "It was time. It's for the best." The rider on course had a rail at the double and Chris pointed to the red, white, and blue oxer, which had a pretty plank with star shapes cut out of it. "That's going to come down a lot. That's the trouble spot."

We watched three more riders before Chris said he better get on. "Are you going to stay and watch?"

"I guess so." I wasn't sure if he wanted me to, but he smiled and said, "Good. You'll bring me luck."

I alternated between watching the riders before him in the order, and sneaking glances at the schooling ring. I felt badly that I wasn't finding out what happened with Dermott, but Jed said he was on it and he knew Zoe best.

Chris was right about the out of the double. The oxer came down in about half of the rounds. The double was tight and most horses couldn't get across the spread of the out without pulling a rail. One girl had torn down the entire jump. Only a few riders had gone clean.

Chris was at the in-gate as his groom wiped Titan's mouth. The rider on course finished up and Chris walked into the ring. Some riders trotted or cantered into the ring. I'd noticed Chris always walked his horses calmly into the ring. Then when the tone sounded, he'd depart into a canter. Titan was a big pure white gelding. He went in a running martingale—which I now knew not only how to identify but how to put on, thanks to Mike—and a gag. Chris made every jump look smooth and unhurried.

He checked Titan back and then rode the combination clear, stopping the clock at 74.39 seconds.

"That's a clean round for Chris Kern and Titan," the announcer said. "They go on the good-list and will return at the end of the class for the jump-off."

Seven riders made it into the jump-off of the twenty-five on the start list. Dermott wasn't one of them. Zoe and Jed hadn't returned and I watched the class alone.

Chris rode the jump-off conservatively, or at least that's what it looked like to me. His time was slow, but he was clear and he ended up in fourth place. After the class was over, I wasn't sure what I was supposed to do. Chris had asked me to watch him. But was I supposed to stay around and see him afterward, or would that be me acting totally dorky? I felt a little more like Zoe with Dermott than I wanted to right then, although I reminded myself I hadn't done anything crazy. All I'd done was say I'd stay and watch him ride.

I glanced over to the in-gate. He was on Titan, walking a

circle around Dale. They were talking about how Titan had gone. I got the feeling from the way they worked together, Dale was more like a friend and almost a co-trainer for Chris.

Chris halted Titan and hopped off. He patted Titan's neck. Dale took the reins from Chris and threw a flysheet over Titan. Then he started back to the barn. I quickly looked back to the ring, pretending to be engrossed in the jump crew taking down the course. I didn't want him to see me staring at him. One of the crew was carrying a pole on his shoulder, like it weighed nothing.

I glanced over again at Chris and it looked like he was walking over to me. My stomach muscles seized up and I told myself to try to remain calm.

"How'd I do?" he asked when he reached me.

"It looked great, but what do I know about jump-offs? It's not like I ever make it past the first round."

"You'll get there," Chris promised. "We've got a bunch more weeks to get you into the jump-offs."

A tractor pulling a trailer came into the ring to swap out some of the jumps.

"If you can do that it'll be a miracle," I said.

"Stop," Chris said. "Don't keep putting yourself down."

I swallowed. "Okay."

Chris looked at me—making sure I understood how serious he was. Someone believed in me. Someone saw potential in me. And it felt great.

# Chapter 14

I FOUND OUT FROM JED that Dermott had given Zoe the total brush off, acting like nothing had happened between them. I guess having sex didn't count for anything in his book. Zoe was devastated and moped around for the rest of the weekend. The only thing that cheered her up a little was the idea of getting me and Nick together Sunday night at Backcountry.

Of course, the only person I cared about seeing that night was Chris. He wasn't there when we arrived and I kept checking the door for him.

Zoe was right. Nick was a nice guy. He had a black lab beagle mix that he'd rescued; he was a huge Minnesota Twins fan; and he wasn't only an announcer—he actually had a good singing voice and had even tried out for American Idol, making it through the first round. He wrote songs in his spare time and used to play in a bluegrass band. He was even kind of cute and I was pretty sure he thought I was pretty, but he was polite and didn't press things. He had a few beers and one time he put his hand on my back, but that was it. Maybe if I'd never crashed into Chris and had met Nick I'd be totally into him and it would have worked out between us. But I guess love, or romance to be dorky about it, was all about timing. The fact was, I had met Chris first and that had changed everything.

The later it got, the more I wanted to go home. It was pretty clear Chris wasn't coming. The sooner I got to sleep, the sooner the morning would come and I'd see Chris again. Being at the bar without Chris was dull, like watching a big class when you didn't care who won. I kept telling Zoe I was tired and wanted to leave. She kept glancing over at Dermott and begging me to stay a little longer.

The night would have been really boring if Jed hadn't kept us entertained with his dead-on impressions of Jamie. He acted out the different stances she had at the in-gate depending on how you'd done in the ring. There was the WTF stance for when you'd made a huge mistake where she spread her legs like a cowboy. There was the I-Train-Her stance for when people like Zoe laid it down where Jamie stood extra tall and sort of raised her chin up to the sky.

Jed knew all Jamie's trademark phrases too like when you walked a course and she told you what number of strides to do in a line. Jed pretended to stride off the distance and then declared, "Seven strides. Or it could be eight. The seven is a definite maybe."

Zoe, Nick, and I burst out laughing.

Jed said, "A definite maybe? What the fuck does that mean?"

Nick added, "At the in-gate she'll come up and say she's got two and she wants to go tenth and eleventh in the order unless something happens and we'll have to readjust. She always says that last part: we'll have to readjust."

"Next time just tell her it's a definite maybe," Zoe said.

"Oh my God, yes!" Jed said. "You have to use that on her and see if she notices. That would be hysterical."

"I'm laughing so hard I'm going to pee my pants," Zoe said. She grabbed my hand. "Come with me to the bog."

"The bog?" I said.

"That's what you-know-who calls it."

You-know-who was at the other end of the bar talking with Heather Daly and Amelia Britton. Zoe had kept an eye on the three of them all night. I had a feeling she'd been laughing even louder at Jed's jokes, hoping Dermott would notice and be jealous of what a good time she was having.

At the mirror, Zoe retouched her make-up. Her cheeks were flushed from rum-and-cokes.

"I wonder where Chris is tonight," I said, trying to be ever so casual about it, like it was something that just flitted randomly across my mind, not something I was constantly wondering.

"Let's text him." Zoe pulled out her phone.

"Really? Do you think we should? I mean it's late and do you even have his number?"

Zoe was typing quickly and then made one final flourish of pressing send. "There, sent!"

"Wait, what did you say?"

"Where are you? Hannah wants to blow you." Zoe leaned toward the mirror to inspect her lipstick.

"What? Zoe!" I grabbed her phone from where she'd put it on the counter. I found her text. All it said was, *where are you? Why aren't you here?*

"I totally got you!" Zoe was laughing moronically.

"That was so not funny."

"You should have seen your face. Seriously though, why don't you send him a naked pic?"

"Oh my God, no. Come on." I wanted out of there before Zoe did anything crazy. Maybe keeping an eye on Dermott all night wasn't such a bad thing because at least it kept her occupied.

Back in the bar, I gave the room another once-over. Still no Chris. We rejoined Jed and Nick. Jed looked tired and I even got the sense that Nick wanted to go home, but was probably just staying because of me. Finally I said, "I really think I'm going to call it a night."

"Me too," Nick said. "I gotta let Zeke out."

"You guys are so lame," Zoe pouted.

We headed to the door. Zoe came along, looking nearly dejected. She would have stayed till closing if Dermott stayed. I was going to try to say something to cheer her up, when someone came up behind us and said, "Boo!"

We all turned. It was Dermott.

"Where are you off to? Night is still young, no?"

"That's what I was trying to tell them!" Zoe said, brightening.

"Stay," Dermott said, throwing an arm around her.

"I really want to go," I told Zoe.

"Need a lift home?" Dermott asked Zoe. "I'll take care of you."

"Great," Zoe said. To us: "See you losers tomorrow." She blew us a kiss and headed back into the bar with Dermott.

"Should we let that happen?" I asked Jed.

He raised exasperated shoulders. "What choice do we have?"

"I guess," I said. We couldn't exactly take her home by force and there would be no convincing her that staying with Dermott wasn't in her best interest. I couldn't believe she would forgive him so quickly.

Jed's car was closest to the door. Nick was waiting, hovering around me, making me kind of nervous about what he thought was going to happen.

Jed winked at me when Nick wasn't looking and got in his car. Nick walked me to my car, being very chivalrous. It was really dark in the parking lot. I talked a lot, hoping that would keep anything else from happening.

"I hope Zoe's okay. Dermott ignores her all night and then boom, out of nowhere, he pounces on her. He must have struck out with Heather and Amelia. Maybe I should go back and check on her—make sure she's okay. She was pretty drunk."

I didn't want to go back in, but I figured it might be good to check on her and that way I could ditch Nick, avoid any awkward moments between us, and go home.

"Do you want me to go with you?"

"No, you don't have to."

"I don't mind."

"You're kind, but no." He *was* kind. He was a nice guy, which made this even worse.

"I guess she'll be okay," I said.

We arrived at my car. Nick put a hand on the car, effectively boxing me in with nowhere to go. It was the boldest thing he'd done so far.

"This was fun," he said.

"Yeah, totally," I said.

I needed to end this politely. But it was harder than I imagined. Why had Zoe gotten me into this mess? Before I could figure out what to do or say, Nick leaned in and kissed me. I didn't really kiss him back, but I didn't stop him either. I'm not sure what he thought. Our kiss had no passion and maybe he sensed that meant I wasn't into him.

When it ended he said, "Well, see you."

I guess if I liked him that was when I would have kissed him again or said something encouraging, but all I said was, "Yeah, see you."

# Chapter 15

I WAS SOON LEARNING THAT Mondays were a day of sleeping off hangovers, regretting mistakes, and gossiping about said mistakes of others. It was also about trips to Rite Aide, Stop and Shop, and getting your nails done. Of course I didn't sleep in. But I didn't care. I had my lesson with Chris. And after I had Logan to take care of. On Mondays, it was just me and the grooms at the show, but I didn't mind. It was kind of nice without the drone of the announcer or the trainers and riders rushing every which way. I had rented time in the temporary paddocks and I sat outside the metal fence and watched as Logan happily rolled, walked around, and then grazed on what little grass was there.

Zoe texted me asking if I wanted to go to the nail place with her. I said sure and I met her at the salon after I was done with Logan. There were three other riders already there. Zoe picked out a color called COME-TO-BED-RED and when she saw me looking at PINKY-PIE she shook her head.

We sat down in the chairs. The women started working

on our cuticles. My nails were short but at least there was something there. Zoe said in a quiet voice, "So did you get lucky with Nick? Are you still pure?"

"Yes, I'm still pure."

"Nothing happened?"

"He kissed me."

When I had seen Chris for our lesson that morning, I had felt strangely guilty for having let Nick kiss me. What if Chris found out? Then there was Nick, whom I hadn't seen yet, but would have to see sooner or later. I'd also been dying to ask Chris why he hadn't gone out Sunday night, but I'd never found the right time.

"That's it? All you did was kiss?"

"Yeah."

"I guess it's a start," Zoe said.

I tried to explain that while Nick was nice I wasn't really into him, but she tried to convince me that I didn't need to be madly in love with him to have a pleasant virginity-ridding experience.

"Let's be honest. You probably won't see him again after Circuit. You're going off to be Smart College Girl and he's going to keep going show-to-show announcing. You'll text for a while and then it'll just fade away."

"Wow, you make it sound so romantic."

Zoe snorted. "Romance is really overrated."

"Are you saying that because of last night? What happened with you and Dermott?"

"No, it was good," Zoe said. "I mean he's really good in bed."

"Wow," I said. I wasn't even sure what "good in bed" meant. Did it mean he was self-assured or good at giving her pleasure? Zoe seemed so much more mature in those ways, but I wasn't sure that was a good thing.

"European men are different," she proclaimed. I wondered if Dermott was her first European man. Probably not.

"How?"

"They know women better."

It all sounded mysterious to me. Zoe might as well have been talking about studying ancient languages.

After our polish dried, we went to lunch at the bagel place and then roamed around the outlet stores. Zoe had expensive taste. I wanted to go to J. Crew, but she wrinkled her nose and took me to Michael Kors, Kate Spade, and Coach. The purses at Kate Spade were so gorgeous and they were more than half-off. We tried them and I fell in love with a blue Hobo style.

"Get it," Zoe said as I looked at myself carrying it in front of the mirror. She had one over her shoulder too. "I'm totally getting this one."

I wondered how she could afford it. I checked the price tag on the one I wanted again, doing the discount math in my head.

"You can't come to the horse show and not buy some nice stuff at the outlets," she said.

My dad had given me a credit card to pay for my expenses and things Logan would need. He probably wouldn't even notice if I bought a bag. I usually did most of my shopping online since Mom didn't like crowded stores or malls. Sometimes when I was in California, Monica would take me shopping. It felt nice to be out shopping with Zoe, trying things on, getting each other's opinions.

"Okay, I'm getting it!" I said.

"Good for you!"

We went into Polo and Vineyard Vines, and Zoe looked at a button-down shirt she thought would look fantastic on Dermott. I thought Chris would look good in it too. I wondered what he was doing today—did he ever go outlet shopping? I would have been lying if I said I hadn't hoped we might run into him in town. I thought about buying my dad or Ryan a shirt, or possible getting my mom something. I'd probably do better to get her something bird-related at Orvis.

We ran into lots of riders in town. Everyone knew Zoe and I felt proud to be her chosen partner in crime. I was a celebrity by association. We went for frozen yogurt and then hugged good-bye when it was time for me to head back to the show to take care of Logan. "This was so much fun," I said. "Thank you."

"Thank you? For what?" Zoe made a face.

"I don't know, for including me, I guess."

"You are too funny sometimes," Zoe said, waving me away with her hand. "See you tomorrow."

# Chapter 16

ZOE WAS SUCH A GOOD RIDER that she had been asked to ride a horse in the first years, which went on Wednesday and Thursday, against all the professionals. Jed and I went to watch her and he had me laughing as we waited for Zoe to come into the ring. It was stereotypical, the comic gay guy, but Jed was hysterically funny. I wondered whether he was funny at school, or more likely, it all came out here where he could be himself. At school he probably worked hard at being invisible.

Joyce Tripp was getting a girl ready for the schooling hunters, which were going in the other ring, and we could hear her voice all the way from where we were sitting.

"Close your eyes," Jed said.

"Why?"

"Just do it. Trust me." When I had them closed he added, "Now listen."

There was Joyce's high-pitched voice. "Oh my God, yes, stay straight, yes, ride it, ride it!"

"Doesn't it sound like she's having sex?" Jed asked.

I giggled as Joyce continued. "Again, just like that. Did you feel that? Amazing!"

I opened my eyes, which were watering from laughing so hard.

"I like to call it the trainer orgasm," Jed said. "Good for Joyce, because you know she's not getting any in real life." He was right, of course. Joyce looked more "country farmer" than 'A' circuit trainer. She wore a short-sleeve plaid shirt, high-waisted jeans, and a straw hat. Her frizzy hair was wild and she was missing a few teeth. Most of the horse show world was filled with beautiful people and then there were the few oddballs like Joyce.

I held up my hand. "Stop it—I'll never be able to think about her again without thinking of her—"

"Having sex?"

"No!" I shuddered at the thought.

"Yeah, because that's just repulsive."

Zoe was finally at the in-gate, getting last minute words from the trainer who had asked her to ride the horse. Zoe nodded and entered the ring. Of all the classes she showed in, Zoe was the best at the hunters, which was why she had been asked to show in a professional division. Horses liked her and jumped well for her. She was a super soft rider and was good with sensitive horses. Given her crazy attitude about life, I would have thought she'd be best at the jumpers where sometimes it paid to go fast and take risks. But it was like the hunters brought out the Zen-side of Zoe. If she could be more like hunter-Zoe outside of the ring I thought she'd be a lot happier.

The horse she rode was a big bay with a beautiful head with a blaze. He had a gorgeous lopey canter and then jerked his knees up and rounded his back over the jumps. Zoe looked amazing on him and was laying down a super trip.

"She's so good," I said as she jumped the single oxer on the side of the ring.

"Yeah, she's got a talent. She'll be a great pro if she can get her personal shit together," Jed said. "That's a big fucking if, of course."

She rode down the last line and finished to applause and whoops from the trainer. Jed and I clapped too.

"Do you think she's okay? I mean, I don't know her very well. Is this normal for her? She seems kind of self-destructive or something."

"Of course she's not okay. And what, do you see a shrink? Self-destructive?

"I *should* see a shrink, but no, I've just kind of been exposed to a lot of shrink talk."

"I see a shrink," Jed said.

I admired Jed. He might be lying to his school, but underneath he wasn't afraid to put it all out there and he seemed comfortable with who he was. I only wished my mom's shrink was able to help her as much. And as for me, I was pretty sure I had no idea who I was. Why hadn't I stopped Nick from kissing me? Did I want to keep a possible understudy for when I finally woke up and realized there was no way Chris and I were happening?

"Yes, she's self-destructive. You know she was sleeping with Harding, right?"

There were certain horse show people that were always

referred to only by their first name. If you didn't know who they were, you were a loser. It was that simple. Whenever I found myself not sure who Tim or Jessica was, I played along like I did. Luckily the only Harding I knew was Harding Beckwith, who had been to the Olympics three times for Britain. To go to the Olympics three times you had to be really good. You also had to be pretty old. I didn't know exactly how old Harding was, but he was old, old. Married-with-kids old. I looked at the in-gate where Zoe was getting ready to go back for her second round.

"Harding? But he's like—"

"A dog?"

"I was going to say really old."

"That too. But he's totally hot. It isn't like she was the first junior he's ever bagged. Please. Hard-on?"

I laughed. I'd never heard Harding called that before.

Zoe entered the ring. She walked for a while before picking up a canter like she knew the judge would wait for her.

"She's at the end of a long line of distinguished and not-so-distinguished guests," Jed continued. "But she was the last straw. Gilly knew about all of his sleeping around, but Zoe was the last straw. She found them together. He used to be more careful, had some respect, but he got really careless. She's filing for divorce. He's trying to get her back. And Gilly is totally making Zoe the villain. Making her out to be a calculated family-wrecker. Everyone knows she was one of many, but somehow that hasn't stopped them from making her out to be awful. Some of the stuff people wrote about her online is just cruel."

I looked at Zoe, who had jumped the first line flawlessly.

The horse went so well for her it took your breath away. "Oh my God, I had no idea." I guess Zoe had been with other European men.

"It's been brutal for her. You'd think she might learn something from the whole experience and reform. Go the nun-route. But instead it's like she's out to prove them all right, and just live up to the slut rep."

Zoe finished her trip. I couldn't quite reconcile the picture I was seeing of her riding the most flawless, beautiful rounds with what Jed had told me. On course she looked like she had it all together, but that so clearly wasn't the case.

She was one of the last few to go and Nick called the jogs. Just hearing his voice made me blush. He had texted me a few times and I'd texted back, but our texts were the equivalent of awkward small talk about nothing, which was how I wanted to keep it.

Zoe was on top in both classes. I found myself staring hard at her as she jogged in and then took the blue ribbons. She was talented and she was pretty and she was smart when she wanted to let herself be. Why did she bring herself down by chasing all these worthless guys? And how could I help her see she was better than that?

\* \* \*

Back at the barn, I put Logan on the crossties and took out the clippers that were packed into my trunk by whoever had packed my trunk. Logan's muzzle had grown a bit of stubble and his ears looked a little fuzzy. I had no idea how to clip them but I figured, how hard could it be?

I did quite well with his muzzle and I was very proud of

myself. I felt so accomplished as I ran the clippers lightly over
his skin, listening to the rewarding sound of the spiny hairs
being zipped off. I was probably feeling too cocky as I got out
my step stool and climbed up by his head. I'm not sure I even
reached for his ear—maybe I held the buzzing clipper up and
he saw it. He thrashed his head hard only once, breaking the
crossties. I had jumped off the step stool, standing back, not
cocky anymore. Logan looked at me as I stood there like he
was thinking hard for a moment. He seemed to be trying to
figure out why I was just standing there stone still and not
grabbing him. And why *was* I just standing there? Because I
was dumb and inexperienced when it came to horses. Any
other person would have been leaping to grab the horse. But
not me. I watched Logan realize I wasn't lunging for him and
I watched as he took off out the barn aisle. I ran after him to
the front of the aisle. He trotted out of the tent, his head and
tail raised with excitement. Then he launched into a canter,
getting further and further away from me.

I wanted to scream, but the words wouldn't come out of
my mouth. Instead I ran to find Mike. Luckily, he was wrapping a horse. "Mike, Logan got loose," I panted.

"Where is he?"

"I don't know. I was clipping him and he broke the
crossties. He took off toward the rings."

As I said the words I started panicking. What if he ran
toward the road? Oh God, oh God. What if a car hit him?

Mike called to another groom to put the horse he was
wrapping away. He grabbed a lead rope and filled a bucket
with grain. Then he took off running. I followed.

As we got toward the jumper rings, I heard the announcer call, "Loose horse. Loose horse headed toward Hunter I."

So he was still on the show grounds. But that didn't mean he wouldn't be heading toward the road. The show grounds had no gate or fence around it. The road that ran alongside it wasn't a highway by any means, but people did drive pretty fast on it.

We tore toward the hunter rings. I looked ahead hoping to see a flash of dark bay. The grain in Mike's bucket rattled as we ran. Mike was pretty fast when he wanted to be and I was so grateful to him for helping me. He helped me all the time, and it didn't seem like it was because of Zoe anymore. He was just a really nice guy. Too bad Zoe couldn't see that.

When we reached the hunter rings, I spotted Logan. He had stopped by the schooling ring, his head held high, looking proud of himself, not panicked. A few of the riders in the schooling ring had come to a halt and one of the in-gate guys was heading toward him.

Mike rattled the grain bucket. I swear Logan swung his head and looked at us. I swear he saw me. I felt like I could hear the thoughts in his head. *Is this upping my game enough?*

I would have laughed if I wasn't still worried his little game would end up with him as road kill. He broke into a trot again, going along the outside of the schooling ring. I bet in his head he was laughing at all of us.

"Loose horse headed to the schooling area of Hunter III," the announcer said.

Logan cantered around the schooling ring and then, of all

things, cantered through the in-gate of Hunter II. There wasn't anyone in the ring—the rider about to go on course had held up.

"Maybe he wants to be a hunter," Mike said.

Logan cantered down the middle of the ring, took a left and headed toward the edge of the ring. He beautifully hopped over the thigh-high fence that encircled the ring, cantered right up to Mike and me, and stopped.

Mike held out the bucket. Logan took a bite of grain. Mike clipped the lead rope onto him. At the sound of the metal clipping shut, I felt my whole body sigh. Logan was safe. The way he had come back to us, going through the ring first, made me feel like Logan had a really funny sense of humor. I'd never realized how much personality horses could have.

"That was quite a performance," Mike said.

I wasn't sure whether he was talking to me or Logan.

"Do you want me to lead him back?" he asked me.

"I'll take him," I said. I gave Logan a pat and he nudged me with his nose as if he was making sure I knew he now had bragging rights, that he had one-upped me big-time.

Mike grinned. "Just hold on tight."

# Chapter 17

AFTER TWENTY MINUTES OF flatwork on Friday morning, Chris started adjusting the two jumps in the middle of the ring. I didn't want to get too hopeful—maybe he was setting something up for a horse he was riding later. But then he pointed to the cross rail. "I'm going to place a ground rail on each side of the jump."

"We're jumping? Really?"

Chris continued, "You won't have to look for a distance to take off from. You don't even need to concentrate on the jump at all, only on the rail on the ground. Remember how we trotted and cantered rails yesterday? Just pretend we're doing that. Ride to the rail, not the jump, okay?"

Chris laid the two rails on either side of the jump, measuring out the distance. "Let's try it."

I urged Logan into a trot.

"Shorten up your reins about an inch, good. Ride the rail, not the jump."

I turned to the jump. Chris kept talking and it was soothing to hear his voice, like a guide showing me the way.

"Stay straight, stay in your heels, right there, eyes up, not down, thinking about the rail. Let Logan worry about the jump."

The rail, I thought to myself. Just think about the rail. Logan looked down at the pole on the ground. At first I thought that would be it, he would look down and then stop, possibly hurtling me over his head. But as he looked down, Chris clucked and said, "leg." I squeezed and he continued over the rail, up over the jump, and across the rail on the other side.

"Very good," Chris said. "He looked at the rail and it took his mind off the jump. Did you feel that?"

I nodded. It had felt nearly civilized.

"Come to it again."

I braced myself for trouble this time, for the first time to have been dumb luck, but Logan was good again.

Chris raised the cross-rail to a small vertical and told me to ride it just the same. Everything felt slow and in control, not raced and imbalanced like usual.

"Let him walk and give him a pat."

I rubbed Logan's neck and scratched along his mane.

"That was really good. How did it feel to you?"

"So much better."

Chris nodded. "We're working on details. On making both you and Logan pay attention to the basics, the fundamentals. No one seems to have done that with either of you. You're like a kid that gets to high school, but can hardly read."

"I can read," I said.

Chris gave me a look like being cheeky was okay, but this

wasn't exactly the place for it. "We're getting somewhere," he said.

"I know," I agreed.

"It'll pay off in the ring soon too."

"I wish you could help me instead of Jamie . . ." I said. "Why don't you teach? You're good at it."

Chris put the vertical up another hole. "Harris doesn't want me taking on clients. I need to focus on his horses."

"Harris is . . .?"

"My sponsor. He owns all my horses."

"You could probably do both, right?"

"Probably. But when you have someone buying you grand prix horses you kind of need to do what they want you to."

We jumped the exercise a few more times. Then Chris checked his phone. Every morning at the end of our lesson he checked his phone. And every morning it became more and more awkward for him to leave. For both of us to go on with our days. It was a good sort of awkward. A feeling of things left unsaid, of moments still to develop.

Today I finally got up the nerve and said, "I didn't see you Sunday night."

"Nah, the last time I went with the plan to get drunk and forget everything and then I didn't even go through with it, so I figured what's the point? I'd just stay home."

What was the point? Well, apparently not seeing me. That didn't seem to matter to him. Every time I hoped there was something between us, then something else happened to slap me in the face and tell me to stop dreaming.

"You went out?" Chris asked.

"Yeah, me, Zoe, and Jed." I decided to leave out the part about Nick.

"Was it fun?"

"Oh, yeah. It was so much fun. Except for the part where Dermott spent the whole night acting like Zoe didn't exist and then at the last minute decided he wanted to, well, you know . . ." Why did I start talking about something to do with sex, only to realize I had no idea how to say it and end up just sounding totally lame?

"Did she go home with him?"

I nodded.

Chris shook his head in a brotherly kind of way.

I circled Logan around him. "Why did you want to get drunk? I mean, what do you need to forget?"

Chris took a moment like he was deciding whether he should open up to me. What he said next surprised me. I expected him to talk about Mary Beth or something to do with his personal life.

"I convinced Harris to buy this horse in Europe last winter. Harris only wanted to buy one horse but I found Titan, and then this second, younger horse that I saw something in. Something others apparently weren't seeing. I thought maybe he was special. Harris finally agreed and bought him and now he keeps having rail after rail. I feel like maybe he's not what I thought he was—maybe I was wrong. He keeps having rails. I can't figure out what's going wrong and Harris is none too happy. Now that Nova's hurt, we could have used the money we spent on that horse to put toward another grand prix horse, so it really looks like a stupid decision on my part."

"Maybe the horse needs more time to develop?" I said, even though I didn't know the first thing about grand prix horses or training. I had no idea what I was talking about, but if Chris saw something in the horse it was hard to believe it wasn't talented.

Chris shrugged. "Harris is coming in two weekends. We're going to talk about whether we should go back to Jürgen and try to trade him back in and take the loss. I think if I had more time with him I might be able to figure out what's not working, but Harris wants things to happen right away. He's not one for patience. I swear that's why Nova got hurt in the first place, but that's a whole other story."

I wanted to hear that whole other story. I wanted to hear anything Chris was willing to tell me. He could tell me how he folded his laundry and it would be amazing. But he said, "Well, enough complaining. I have to go ride."

I knew Chris often rode his horses twice a day for fitness. Horses of that caliber were like professional athletes themselves, everything about their health was expertly planned out and managed.

"It's not complaining," I said.

"You're right. I just don't get to unload much—thanks for listening."

\* \* \*

Walking back through the grounds usually took five minutes. Lately I had begun to let Logan amble on a loose rein. His need to race-walk had decreased and he actually walked halfway normally and I felt I could give him his head. Sometimes I took the long route, passing by the rings and the vendors, including Alison, the woman who sold the gorgeous horse-themed jewelry, the show photographer, and the videographer. Most of the vendors' booths were still closed up but there was always the chance someone would be getting ready for the day. Maybe I wanted someone to find out about the lessons. Then it would be real. But it would also be trouble for me if Jamie found out, and probably for Chris too with Harris.

I put Logan away in his stall and threw him his morning grain. He gobbled it up and started in on his hay.

It was only a little after seven o'clock, but it felt more like nine or ten. I cleaned Logan's stall and then went up to the food truck to get something to eat. I ended up running into Jed, who was going to watch Zoe show a new ride in the jumpers. I went with him and didn't get back to the stalls until an hour later. Logan gave me a heart attack because at first I didn't see him in his stall and I thought he'd escaped and was running around the horse show again. But he was just lying down.

"I know how you feel," I told him as I peered in on him. I would have liked to go back to the condo and climb into bed.

I looked at Logan a moment longer. Somehow he didn't look totally relaxed. His eyes were worried and he was blowing hard through his nose.

"Are you okay?" I asked him.

He made a funny kind of groan that I'd never heard from him before. Something didn't seem right. I opened the door and he didn't even try to get up. Then he curled his neck to bite at his stomach. Was he colicking? I'd heard about horses colicking and even having colic surgery, but I'd never actually seen a horse colicking. If I'd spent more time in the barn, I would have but I'd only ever been in the barn a few minutes while a groom was getting my horse ready.

I felt all panicky looking at Logan. He looked miserable and it was awful to see him in pain. What if he was really in bad shape? How had it happened so fast? I thought back to my lesson. He'd seemed fine then, and fine when I'd brought him back. I checked his water buckets. There was water in them. I hadn't forgotten to fill them. So what the hell had I done wrong?

I ran over to Jamie's stalls and found Mike organizing the tack room. "Can you come over and look at Logan? I think he's sick."

Mike hustled over with me. He made Logan stand up and put his ear against his side. "I hear some gut sounds, not tons but some, so that's good."

He snapped a lead rope on him and led him out of the stall. "We need to get him walking. We don't want him to twist up."

I nodded like I knew what he was saying. Twist up? In fact, I didn't know what it meant, but it didn't take an expert in horse care to know it was bad.

"Yeah. Did he seem okay this morning?"

"He was fine. I took him for a hack, brought him back."

Logan didn't want to walk and Mike made him. He spoke softly to him, encouraging him. To me he said, "Just a hack? Did you work him hard? Was he sweating?"

Fear gripped me deep inside. What had I done? It was bad

enough that I was lying since I'd had a lesson. "He was sweat-ing a little."

"When did you feed him? Was he cooled down enough?"

I kept pace with Mike. "I fed him after I hacked him."

"How long after? Right after?"

"I don't know. Ten minutes, maybe."

Mike shook his head. "You have to feed a while after. Like at least forty-five minutes. What were you doing riding so early anyway?"

"Oh no, I did this," I said, ignoring his question.

"You didn't know," Mike said.

"Is he going to be okay?"

Mike stopped and Logan immediately nipped at his side. "We better get the vet."

Seriously? I'd had enough of Logan upping his game. Pooping in his water buckets hadn't been enough, nor had nearly galloping across Route 8A and getting hit by a car. Now he had to colic . . .

# Chapter 18

THE HORSE SHOW VET ARRIVED ten minutes later. Mike was still making Logan walk as I paced next to them, freaking out that I'd seriously endangered my horse. Would my dad pay for colic surgery? Probably, but Mike said the nearest vet hospital was Cornell, over four hours away. By the time Logan got there it could be too late to save him. What would happen if he died? Would that be it for my riding? Would I pack up and spend the rest of the summer at home before going to college? Only a few weeks ago, that wouldn't have sounded like a bad option, although I didn't exactly want to spend the summer stuck home with Mom and her birds. But now, Logan was showing signs of improvement. I was actually liking riding for the first time since Dobby and well, there was Chris.

Doc Sheridan was from Florida but he spent the circuit as the official horse show vet for a nice working vacation. He was calm and talked in a voice barely louder than a whisper. He seemed the complete opposite of the vet we used at home who also catered to horses on the circuit. That vet rushed through everything, always talking about the next barn he had to get to.

Doc Sheridan listened to Logan's stomach with his stethoscope and felt around with his hands. He put on rubber gloves that went all the way up to his elbows and stuck his hand up Logan's rectum, pulling out manure. He did that without even wrinkling his nose when I had to cover my mouth with my hand and look away.

"Don't be so squeamish," Mike said.

Doc Sheridan peeled off his gloves. "Things are still moving in there so I'm not overly concerned. I'd like to give him some Banamine and see if we can get him to work through this on his own."

"So he's not going to die?" I blurted out.

"I sure hope not." Doc moved to his truck and took out a needle and syringe. He filled it up with Banamine and Mike held Logan while he injected him in a vein on his neck just under his throatlatch.

Zoe came over while we were waiting to see if the Banamine was going to help. "I heard he's colicking."

I nodded, grateful that she didn't say something about how she'd heard it was because I'd fed him at the wrong time.

After a few minutes Logan stopped pecking at his sides. His overall expression seemed more relaxed.

I wasn't sure if Zoe was purposely trying to distract me when she whispered, "I am so fucking pissed. I just saw Dermott and he acted like there was nothing between us again," but I was glad to think about something else for a moment besides how I had put my horse's life at risk with my own negligence.

"What did he say to you?"

"Hey, Zoe." Zoe shook her head. "Which is fine with me because as far as I'm concerned nothing did happen and that DB can screw whoever he wants."

Doc held his stethoscope up to Logan's side again. "Better gut sounds. Do you want to have a listen?" He was looking at me.

"Me?"

"You're the horse's mom, aren't you?"

Our vet at home never wanted clients to have anything to do with examinations. He certainly never referred to the clients as moms of the horses. He preferred to deal with Jamie. Here Doc was asking me to participate?

"Um, okay." Doc passed me the stethoscope. I held it to Logan's stomach. I heard gurgles kind of like underwater dolphin language without the high-pitched noises.

I stood up and took off the stethoscope. "That's his . . .?"

"That's his intestines working properly. You want to hear lots of noise in there. If it's silent it means the system is shutting down and intestines in horses die very quickly if they're not functioning. You can actually hear it without a stethoscope too. Put your ear up against his side."

I pressed my ear to Logan's belly like Mike had done. I could hear the same noises, just less pronounced.

"I want you to keep a close eye on him all day. Take a listen and make sure you hear digestion going on in there. Has this horse ever colicked before?"

"No, not that I know of." I was sure we were going to get to what had caused this episode.

"Hopefully this is a one-time incident, but make sure you're taking him out for lots of walks, and feed him hay before his meals to line his stomach. Is he on Gastroguard?"

"No," I said. I had seen the tubes around the barn at home and maybe Logan had been on it before coming to Vermont. But besides a few last remaining trays from SmartPak, nothing else had been sent with him. It was another black mark against my barn management that I hadn't asked what supplements and treatments I should be giving him. Mike had told me when he needed to be shod, but what else had I missed?

Doc went into his truck and handed me a few tubes of Gastroguard. "Ask Mike where to get more," he said.

\* \* \*

The rest of the day, I did what Doc Sheridan said and I kept a close eye on Logan. I didn't leave my stalls except to go to the bathroom. He looked completely recovered, eating his hay happily. Mike came over and checked on Logan and I quizzed him about what supplements Logan should be taking and where to get more Gastroguard. He told me the best thing to do was to buy it in bulk online.

Chris came by later in the afternoon. I was sitting on my tack trunk listening to music on my iPhone. He took me by surprise because I didn't know he even knew where my stalls were. Perhaps he'd asked Zoe or maybe it was obvious that I'd be stabled next to Jamie.

"I heard Logan was colicking."

"He's okay now."

Chris peered in his stall. "That's good to hear." He came to sit down next to me on my tack trunk. He was suddenly very close to me. "What are you listening to?"

"My brother makes me these playlists. He's got good taste in music."

"You don't?"

"I don't know. He's just better at those kinds of things."

"He's older than you?"

"Yeah, he's . . . awesome. I don't know what I'd do without him."

"I feel the same way about my brother. When your parents get divorced it's nice to have someone who gets it all."

"Exactly. Although my brother gets along with my father. They're kind of more alike."

"So, Zoe wants us all to go out for dinner tonight. Take her mind off Dermott."

I looked over my shoulder at Logan. "I don't think I can. I mean, I'm pretty much scared to leave his side. I might have to sleep here." I wasn't exaggerating. Logan being sick had scared me in a way I'd never thought possible. Maybe it was because he was going better, or maybe it was because I was taking care of him all by myself, but I felt like I actually liked him now. Maybe even somewhat loved him. Like Doc Sheridan had said, I was his mom. Logan didn't have anyone else in the world but me. He depended on me. "He colicked because of me."

Chris looked confused.

"I fed him too soon after our lesson."

"You can't be sure that's what did it."

"But he's never colicked before."

"As far as you know . . ."

Chris had a point. Logan could have colicked before without Jamie telling us.

"He's fine now. You can come back after dinner and check on him."

I looked at Logan again, happily munching his hay.

Chris wasn't one to be careless when it came to horses. If he thought it was okay to leave Logan for a few hours, it was probably okay.

# Chapter 19

I SHOWED UP AT THE MEXICAN place Zoe had picked and walked inside. Chris was already there and so were Zoe, Jed, and Nick. Nick? I could have killed Zoe. She had said it was going to be Jed, me, and Chris. Now I had to sit at a table with the guy I liked who didn't know I liked him and the guy I didn't like who didn't know I didn't like him and somehow that was supposed to work out okay? What if Zoe said embarrassing things about trying to get me and Nick together in front of Chris?

I gave Zoe the evil eye, but she either chose to ignore me or had no idea what I was trying to convey to her.

"Hey," Nick said. "Great to see you. I kept looking for you all week to come by and say hi at least."

"I don't get to hunter land often," I said, glancing at Chris to see if he had detected anything strange going on between Nick and me.

Nick looked so dorky and terrible in comparison to Chris. I felt bad thinking it, but he was five inches shorter than Chris and somehow looked very short and stubby standing next to him. He had his khakis rolled up at the bottom and a belt that looked so worn he might have used it half the time as a leash for his dog. And he was wearing a T-shirt from another horse show that said STAFF on the back. Chris, however, wore perfectly fitting khakis, a nice braided belt, and a Vineyard Vines polo shirt.

The hostess came and told Chris our table was ready. Even she seemed to know he was the one to talk to of all of us, the most adult and in-charge.

We followed her to the table and I had no choice but to sit next to Nick. The restaurant had cute décor with colorful plates and fake dried peppers on the walls. The tabletops were made of tiles in shades of burnt orange and umber. It was loud and half the horse show was there. I knew I would have been having a great time if Nick wasn't there.

"So are you having a good week?" Nick asked.

"Yeah, it's fine," I said.

"I texted you yesterday to see if you wanted to hang out after the show was over. A few of my buddies from the crew were going to kick back at the Cave with a few beers. Did you get that text?"

The Cave was where the jump crew kept the tractors, water trucks, extra standards, and rails. It was home base for them. I knew a lot of girls would have loved to get an invitation to hang out at the Cave. But I wasn't one of them.

I was acutely aware that Chris was listening to all of this. I wasn't sure, but it seemed like he was trying to figure out what was up between Nick and me. He would know that getting invited to the Cave meant something was going on. Maybe Zoe had already told him that we were together or had kissed or were almost together. The thought made my stomach ache.

"Um, yeah, I got it. I just, I had a bunch of stuff to do."

"Like what?" Nick asked.

"College stuff. Like we have to fill out all these forms online. Pre-registration." I thought that was a pretty good lie. It sounded legit to me, anyway. I had no idea I could be so good at coming up with a lie like that right on the spot.

"Oh, yeah, that's cool. Where are you going again?"

"Tufts in Boston."

"I went to a semester of college," Nick said. "But it wasn't for me."

He just wouldn't stop talking. God, I wanted somehow to make the conversation include all of us, not just me and him. And did he think this was impressing me? Talking about dropping out of college to announce horse shows?

I didn't know how to change what was happening. This would have been so different if Nick wasn't here. I would have been talking to Chris. I was so desperate for something to change things that my heart leapt when I saw Dermott pass our table with a blonde in a maxi dress and strappy sandals, even though I knew it would kill Zoe.

Zoe saw Dermott and Dermott saw Zoe.

"Oh no," she said under her breath. "You've got to be shitting me."

Suddenly even Nick was quiet. I don't think any of us really knew what to do or what to say. Dermott gave this slight kind of cool nod. He didn't seem embarrassed or ashamed of his behavior. He just kept walking.

Zoe turned her face away. "Jessica Pellegrini? Seriously? He's here with that slut?"

Even worse, the table the hostess led them to was diagonally across from us. There was no escaping looking at them.

"Just pretend like they aren't even here," Jed said. "Let's get some sangria."

"Right," Chris said. "Sangria and nachos." He signaled to a passing waiter and asked for fully loaded nachos and a pitcher of sangria.

"I think I lost my appetite," Zoe said. "But I could drink."

"What horses are you doing tomorrow?" Chris asked her, clearly trying to take her mind off Dermott.

"Tomorrow, tomorrow." Zoe tried to focus. "Um, I have one in the High Junior Jumper Classic and one in the lows. Two junior hunters."

"Which horse do you have going in the Highs?"

"Bliss."

"I've seen him go. He's got some scope. Where did he come from?"

Not far enough away from us, Jessica was leaning close to Dermott. She laughed at something he said and then pulled her blond hair back, revealing her neck. I couldn't help but think of birds and their courtship rituals. The fact that I knew about bird courtship fell into the category of knowledge-you-wish-you-didn't-have. It was one of the things Mom liked to talk about and even if I wasn't exactly listening, I would nonetheless absorb. There were plenty of things I tried hard to learn and remember and couldn't, yet without even trying I knew this useless information.

Jessica laughed her high-pitched laugh and then ran her fingers through her hair.

Birds courted their mates in different ways depending on the species. Some sang to get another bird's attention. Some preened themselves or their would-be mate. Others did dramatic head-dips and wing-flaps. Still more offered their desired-one food or built them a nest. Usually it was the male bird that did most of the elaborate courting and the female decided whether she liked him or not. Jessica was the one who was doing the courting here—the head dip, the preening, the singing. Just as I was thinking about this she reached out to Dermott with her drink and offered him a sip.

Even though she shouldn't, Zoe was watching all of this. It would have been nearly impossible to look away. And it was probably like a commercial for a gruesome horror-flick—you had to look, even though you knew it would be awful. She certainly wasn't thinking of bird mating rituals, but like anyone in the restaurant that night she could tell where this was heading.

The waiter brought the pitcher of sangria and Zoe poured herself a glass right away. Chris suggested we order our main courses and I think he was thinking what we all were—how can we speed this disaster meal up and get the hell out of here? I ordered chicken fajitas. Zoe couldn't really think straight and Jed ordered for her. He put his arm around her and said, "It's gonna be all right."

I had to hand it to Chris. He came up with endless things to talk about to keep Zoe from totally falling apart as Dermott and Jessica continued their mating dance. He asked Zoe which horse she was going to ride in the eq finals and what she was thinking of doing after she finished up as a junior. Somehow, mercifully, time went by. I don't know about anyone else but I barely tasted my food. Between Dermott and still feeling uncomfortable with Nick sitting next to me, looking at me all hopeful, I just wanted to be done too and get out of there. I also kept thinking about Logan and hoping he was okay.

We left before Dermott and Jessica. In the parking lot, I was super glad that Jed and Zoe had come together.

"Will you take care of her?" I asked Jed.

"Of course. She'll be okay."

I wished Nick would have gotten in his car and left already, but of course he was lingering around. Jed and Zoe headed to Jed's car and that left Nick, me, and Chris standing there awkwardly. Could this get any worse?

"Well, I should go check on Logan," I said, desperately looking for my exit plan.

Nick moved to stand next to me, leaving Chris across from us. It was only two or three steps, but it was like a bird's mating dance, like an animal staking its territory. Those few steps and maybe the way Nick was looking at Chris said epic amounts. They said, *I'm into her. There's something between us. And you're the third wheel that doesn't belong, so scram.*

Chris seemed to understand all that. I thought I saw surprise, or maybe even disappointment, in his eyes. I wanted to explain it all to him right then and there—to tell him there was nothing between Nick and me whatsoever.

"All right, you kids have a good night," Chris said, and then he turned and left.

His words stabbed me. *You kids.* That was what he thought I was—a kid. And maybe I was a kid, the way I was blundering everything. But one thing was perfectly clear to me right then. Even if Chris wasn't interested in me, I wasn't interested in Nick. If I couldn't have the real thing, I didn't want the imposter.

"I think Zoe gave you the wrong idea," I told Nick.

"What do you mean?"

"Did she say I wanted a boyfriend or something?"

"No, she said she thought you and I might be good together."

"I'm not saying this right," I said. "I'm not really looking for a relationship . . ." Ugh, that wasn't true. I was looking for a relationship. Just not with Nick. I had never even dated anyone and now it was like I was fast-forwarding to the break up part. Maybe I was making this too complicated. That would be just like me.

"I have to go check on Logan," I said.

"Yeah, okay," Nick said.

The look on his face said it all. He got it now. Whatever I had said or not said had made my feelings known.

"I'll see you around," he mumbled.

I wanted to kick my car tires and bang the steering wheel. I had scared Chris away for sure because he thought Nick and I were together and I'd been like a tease to Nick, who wasn't a bad guy. Instead I started the car and drove over to the show. I couldn't wait to see Logan. Suddenly everything about Logan seemed so much simpler. I would pick out his stall, put on his sheet, make sure he was feeling okay. There was such comfort in all those little things I now knew how to do. And there would be comfort in Logan's smell, his nuzzling my hair as I tried to squeak by him with the pitchfork.

The show grounds were dark and quiet, just one or two trucks parked outside the tents. All the vendors' trailers were closed up and the food tent had its flaps down. The quiet and calm was just what I needed. All the horses had their heads low, resting or picking at hay. Logan was dozing and raised his head, surprised to see me.

"You feeling okay, buddy?" I opened his stall door and traced my hand from his neck, over his back. He looked fine, but I put my ear to his stomach like Doc Sheridan had taught me. Even without the stethoscope I heard lots of rumblings and grumblings in there. For once I was glad to see plenty of manure in his stall, even if it meant I needed to pick it out. I checked Logan's water buckets. One was half-full which meant he was drinking. And there was no poop in the bucket . . .yet. Maybe his plan was to drink out of his buckets all night and then poop in them right before I arrived. I smiled at the idea of him being crafty like that.

I picked his stall clean and threw him another flake of hay. I put his light sheet on, making sure all the buckles were done up just right. Before I left, I went back into the stall one more time to pat Logan and kiss him goodnight. I ended up throwing my arms around him, something I'd never done before. I hugged him tight, for the first time ever grateful to have him in my life.

As I was getting into my car, I looked up at the road going by the horse show. I didn't know what made me look. There was a car parked parallel to my tent. I squinted to make out the kind. It sure looked like an Acadia—the kind of SUV Chris drove. But it wouldn't be Chris, would it? He had gone home. Why would he be hovering near my barn? Unless he was checking on me. To see whether I needed help with Logan? Or to see if I was alone, whether Nick had come with me?

I felt like someone in the car was watching me. When I got to my own car and started the engine, the SUV pulled back onto the road and disappeared.

# Chapter 20

CHRIS TEXTED ME LATER that night to say he wasn't going to be able to teach me in the morning. I wanted to write back so many things. Like, why? Why can't you teach me? Will you ever teach me again? Or, there's nothing between me and Nick. Even, was that you at the show grounds watching me? Of course instead, I just wrote back, "okay, thanks."

\* \* \*

I woke up early the next morning, even though I didn't need to be up since I had no lesson. I decided to go to the show early anyway because I was afraid I'd find Logan in pain, or worse. But he was there, happily looking up at me. I gave him his hay first and only after he'd eaten a bunch and lined his stomach did I give him his grain.

I hated not seeing Chris all morning and I was grateful to have Logan to take care of. I spent an extra long time cleaning his stall and scrubbed out his water buckets twice, even though he hadn't pooped in them. I still had too much time after I was done so I flatted him, trying to work on everything Chris has taught me. Then I gave him a nice bath and grazed him while he dried. Grazing our horses was something none of us at Jamie's barn ever did and I had discovered it was one of my favorite things. I loved how happy it made Logan and I loved watching as he negotiated the grass with his lips, picking out just the sections he wanted. He particularly loved clover and dandelions and he was like a surgeon with his dexterity—I swear he could pick up one single blade of grass if he wanted to.

At noon the announcer's voice boomed over the show grounds. "We are set for a one o'clock start out on the grand prix field with the $30,000 Green Mountain Grand Prix. The course is now open to walk."

Those were the words I'd been waiting all day for. My invitation to see Chris. I threw Logan a flake of hay and went up to the ring to watch. I settled into the stands next to a few other riders and some spectators. Signs from sponsors of the circuit lined the fence of the ring—Purina, Equifit, the Weathersville Inn—and flags from different countries hung from the stands. A few pretty trees had been planted next to the ring and were encircled with beds of colorful flowers. There were six pre-teen girls from a sleep-away horse camp. They all wore pink shirts that said HORSE CRAZY on the front and BRAE CASTLE CAMP on the back.

There was a breeze today, which kept the temps cool. Chris was wearing his team USA windbreaker. He looked so amazing and it killed me all over again that if there had been a glimmer of hope that he might like me, seeing me with Nick had killed it.

Chris talked with Tommy Kinsler, another rider, pointing out over the course, going over how to ride it.

The announcer said, "Ten minutes and counting before our start time for the grand prix. The riders will finish up their course walk and we'll have our first in the ring right at one o'clock."

More spectators filled the stands, including a mother with two young girls in pretty yellow and pink sundresses and cotton cardigans. The girls looked at the jumps with wide eyes. In the warm-up ring, the first few riders were schooling. Classes continued in the other rings at the show, but there was a tension in the air at the grand prix ring. This was the biggest class of the week—the class that the grand prix riders had trained for all week.

Chris finished walking the course and was standing near the in-gate. He must have drawn later in the class. Zoe came and found me. She sat down and put her head on my shoulder. "Ugh, that sucked last night, seeing Dermott."

"I know," I said. "It was icky."

She raised her head back up. "Did anything more happen with you and Nick? I saw him at hunter land today, but he brushed me off."

"Zoe, he's really not my type. I mean, he's a good guy and he's cute . . ."

"I know, which is why he's perfect to relieve you of your precious chastity."

"I don't know," I said.

"So you don't want to give him your gift? I thought you wanted to be rid of your burden."

Burden, gift. Which one was it? Being a virgin was totally confusing. "What about *you* and Nick?" I said. "I just think you deserve someone nice. Someone good for you. Someone who'll be good *to* you."

"You mean unlike the pride of the Irish, or are you talking about Hard-on?"

"You're too good for guys like that. You have so much to offer."

Zoe gave me a look. "You sound like a mother. Not *my* mother, but *a* mother."

"I'm serious. You need to value yourself more."

Zoe rolled her eyes. "Now you sound like Jed. I'm just having a little fun."

"It didn't look like fun last night."

"You're sweet." She took my arm. "You're sweet to care about me."

"I do care. And you should be better to yourself."

"Okay, I'll try."

"Starting with Nick?"

Zoe winked at me. "No, honey, that bull is all yours to ride."

"That's not happening," I said. "I pretty much told him last night it wasn't, you know . . . there was no spark."

"No spark, huh?" Zoe said.

"Like what you said about losing your virginity . . . You were attracted to T.J., right? I mean he was nice, but you were still attracted to him?"

"Yeah, I was."

"I'm just not attracted to Nick."

Zoe nodded like this she could finally understand. "Okay, he's not your type. I get it. We're learning together what your type is. It's not Nick. Maybe it's the show crew thing. You need someone a little more intellectual." Zoe looked out over the show grounds like she was thinking hard. "I don't have it yet, but I'll find someone else."

Well, I had gotten Zoe off the Nick-thing. But it wouldn't be long till she found someone else to push on me. I took a quiet breath, trying to savor whatever little time I had before she landed on my next set-up. Maybe I'd be so lucky as to at least watch the grand prix in peace.

Sandy McKay was the first to go in the class. No one ever wanted to go first and Sandy was young. She had been a top junior rider and now went to Princeton. She was new to the grand prix ranks, had three nice horses, and a private trainer. Zoe had told me that her father, a software mogul, had promised her trainer a million-dollar bonus if she made the short list for the next Olympic games.

Sandy looked nervous—her arms and back stiff. But her horse was a seasoned grand prix horse that had been part of the Swiss team at the World Equestrian Games. He marched her around the course. He was clear till the triple combination when she got jumped loose and he pulled the back rail of the last oxer. He had one more rail down for eight faults. Sandy patted his neck gratefully as she came out.

Next was Eve Benzinger. She was barely over five-feet tall and always seemed to be riding giant horses. Somehow she made it work, controlling them despite her tiny size. Today she was on a huge chestnut gelding. He wore an elaborate bit that looked like a mix between a Pelham and a hackamore. I didn't know what the bit was called but at least now I could identify a Pelham and a hackamore. She cruised around the course, turning in a clear round. It was ten more rounds until another totally clear round. By the time Chris was on deck, two others had gone clean, including Dermott. I had decided that the main trap of the course was the triple combination. The distance between the first and second jumps was long and the distance between the second and third short. To execute it well a horse had to jump into the first part with enough speed to make it in one stride and then be able to slow down in time to make the two strides fit in before the last jump. Most riders had rails at the second and third efforts and a few had gotten so wound up to jump in forward to the in that they had botched it and had a rail there too.

At the in-gate Chris was calm and composed as he gazed out over the course. I stared at him, wanting him so badly. Wanting him to like me. Wanting us to be together. The rider on course exited the ring to light applause and Chris legged Titan in.

"We now welcome into the ring Titan and Chris Kern. Titan is a seven-year old, 16.2 hand Mecklenburg gelding owned by Harris Delaney and the Willow Edge Farm of Elizabethtown, Pennsylvania."

Chris walked down the far side of the ring, waiting for the signal that the timer was reset. When the tone sounded, he picked up a canter immediately and headed toward the first jump without even circling. I had seen Chris riding "Buddy" around the show the other day. He was an impressive looking horse, with the cresty neck and proud head of a stallion, even though he was a gelding. Maybe he had been gelded late. Chris looked great too—his breeches, which were the required white for the grand prix, stood out against his navy jacket with the white shirt and tie.

Chris sailed over the first five jumps of the course, checking Buddy back on the landing side and then moving forward again. He rode the whole course on a measured stride, in control and smooth. On the turn to the final combination, the crowd became silent. Chris legged Buddy into a steady hand like he had taught me to do with Logan. Buddy surged forward, meeting the first effort of the combination on a forward stride but still in control. Chris landed from the jump, pressed Buddy forward for half a stride to make sure he would be at the next jump in time, and then steadied back. Buddy gave a tremendous jump over the second oxer, rounding his back and lifting his hind end almost as high as the jump standards.

On the landing side, Chris said, "whoa," as he sat back in the saddle, shortening Buddy up for the two last strides and then legging him up over the last oxer. When Chris landed, the crowd applauded loudly. As he bent down to pat Buddy, the announcer said, "And that makes five coming back for our jump-off with six more riders to see in the class. Chris Kern and Titan have a clean go with 78.89 on the clock for no time faults."

Unlike my classes, where the riders jumped-off immediately if they cleared the course to save time for the show, for the grand prix the jump-off was always run at the end of the class to add excitement. I had never cared so much about watching a grand prix before. This might as well have been a World Cup or Olympic qualifying class given how much I wanted Chris to win.

Dermott came into the ring for his second ride and Zoe and I put the hex on him. It didn't work, however, as he rode a clean round.

As the last few riders went, Chris got back on Buddy. He trotted and cantered around the schooling area, flexing Buddy to the inside and then the outside. I hoped Zoe wasn't noticing how much I was watching Chris, or how I looked at him when he was in the ring. I think she was so consumed with trying not to care about Dermott that she wasn't paying much attention to me.

I noticed Dale trying to flag Chris down. He held out a cell phone.

Chris kept cantering and shook his head.

I wondered who could be calling that Dale would even consider interrupting him at a time like this? And what did it mean that Chris had waved him off? Could it have been Mary Beth calling from Europe, messing up the timing because of the time change? But why would Dale tell Chris she was calling? Unless she was still that important to him.

I told myself to stop the insanity. For all I knew, it could be his mom or dad calling. But wouldn't they know that 2:30 on grand prix day was a bad time to call?

There was one more clear round to bring the jump-off to seven. The last horse finished the course and there were a few minutes of course adjustments before the jump-off began. The two girls in sundresses were getting restless and their mother pointed out the riders jumping in the schooling ring.

The announcer went over the jump-off route, which was seven fences and included an inside option to a big oxer and a long gallop to a tall skinny vertical. I wondered whether Chris would choose the inside turn.

Chris pulled up in the schooling area to watch Eve, the first to go. She was known to be a speed demon and went all out, even though she was the first to go. She took the inside turn and flew to the last jump, finding a long distance to the skinny. Her horse ticked the rail with his front hooves and it rattled in the cups, but didn't come down.

"A very fast first round. Seraphina 7 and Eve Benzinger finish with no faults and a time of 31.75."

I alternated between watching Chris school over one more jump and watching Dermott on his first horse. Of course, he went all out. Angling jumps, turning in the air, galloping when he could. Thankfully he got in a little deep to one of the verticals and had a rail. His time was incredibly fast but the four faults would cost him the win. When Chris entered the ring, there were two clears with Eve still in the lead, Dermott with four faults, and one eight-faulter. Eve would be hard to beat. To do it, Chris would really have to fly. And there were still two to go after Chris, including Dermott again.

Chris picked up a canter and pressed Buddy forward. He was approaching the first jump at a good clip, but it was still hard to tell whether he would go for it. I snuck glances at the clock to see if I could tell how fast he was going. He seemed fast, but perhaps a second or two slower than Eve. After the third jump, he chose not to make the inside cut to the oxer and I could feel the crowd give a collective sigh. He was clearly choosing not to try to beat Eve. He galloped the last jump, but not in a reckless way, finishing with a time two seconds slower. He patted Buddy and left the ring looking pleased.

Dermott went next and again he flew around the course. This time he had the last jump down. Zoe and I shared a pleased look. Todd Gabriel was last to go. I silently willed him to have a rail down and he did, when he made the inside turn to the oxer.

"Four faults and a time of 34.56 which will put Todd Gabriel and Archangel in fourth place. We'll have the full results and award presentation coming right up."

I watched the award presentation even though the crowd thinned out and I was only one of the few people left in the stands, along with the camp girls. Zoe had gone back to the barn, saying she'd catch up with me later. Chris took off his helmet to accept the red ribbon and the camp girls learned close and tittered about him. I could make out the words "totally hot" and "gorgeous." Once he was out of the ring, Chris dismounted and handed Buddy to Dale. He took off his helmet and put it under his arm, stopped to take a drink from a water bottle, and Dale handed him his phone.

I headed back to the barn. I picked out Logan's stall, raked the aisle, and made the grain for that night and tomorrow morning. Then I sat around feeling agitated. All I could think was Chris, Chris, Chris.

So my options were to spend the rest of the day and night thinking about him and wondering what was going on. Or, to go talk to him. Before I could chicken out, I headed over to Chris's barn. Halfway there I almost turned around, but I made myself keep going.

His barn was the first two aisles of the first tent, the part that looked out onto the front of the show grounds—the horse show equivalent of high priced real estate. Barns and riders were given tent locations based on their prominence. Olympic contenders got the first tent or two—no-name trainers were relegated to the back forty. The first aisle was well decorated with navy blue and gray curtains that said Willow's Edge Farm in big letters across them. A few banners from Chris's sponsors—Equifit and Adequan—hung on the side of the tent. There were pots of red geraniums lining the stalls and two of the front stalls had been converted into a sitting area with wood chips spread on the floor, director's chairs, a coffee table, and a photo of Chris sailing over a huge jump. Chris was sitting there, looking at something on his phone. A big white dog was sitting next to him.

"Hi," I said.

He looked up. "Oh, hi."

I think he actually looked happy to see me. Surprised, but happy.

"You rode great," I said.

"Not great enough, apparently."

"What do you mean?"

Chris hadn't put his phone away. He held it up like *it* was the problem. "Harris watched the video stream of the grand prix. He wanted me to go all out and now he's pissed I didn't win. But the horse needed that confidence builder."

"Was that him calling you before the jump-off?" I said, blurting it out without realizing it made it look like I was scrutinizing his every move.

"Yup. If I didn't take the call, he couldn't tell me what to do, but now it's bad enough that I didn't answer *and* I didn't win."

"I'm sorry," I said. "That sucks."

"So what's up?" he said. "Did you need something?"

"Um, I guess I just wondered why this morning didn't happen?"

"Oh, I just, I needed to be concentrating on the grand prix. Saturdays are tough, you know."

"Sure," I said. "I get it. Okay." I put my hands in my pockets. Was that it? Was I supposed to walk away?

Dale came out and said, "All set, boss." He gave me a sideways glance, like he didn't like that I might be messing with Chris's state of mind. I had heard more about Dale from Zoe. Dale had worked for the barn Chris rode with as a junior and he had become like a combination of Chris's older brother and a guardian. Chris's parents couldn't go on the road all the time so Dale essentially took care of Chris. Over the years their relationship had changed and developed, and now Dale was his barn manager. Zoe said Dale was the person that besides his parents Chris trusted most in the world. He was his go-to person for advice on horses . . . and life.

"Okay, so you're going to hardware store," Chris said.

"Guess so," Dale said, not budging.

"Good, see you later."

Dale eyed me again and then left.

"Hey, can I see the horse you were talking about? The one you picked out in Europe?" I asked Chris.

"Sure." Chris stood up and led me down the aisle. The white dog followed, staying close to Chris. "This is Jasper," Chris said.

I patted Jasper but he didn't seem very interested in affection from anyone else besides Chris.

Each of Chris's horses had a stall and a half, a real luxury. His barn was immaculate with sheets neatly hung on the stall doors and beautiful leather halters with shiny nameplates.

"This is him," Chris said. "Arkos."

I had to stand close to Chris in order to look in the stall. The horse was a big bay with a thick mane and tail. He noticed us looking and poked his nose through the slats of the door. I put my finger through the slats and touched his nose. He was super friendly.

Chris reached over me to unlock the stall door and when I turned away from Arkos, it was like he was blocking me against the stall door by accident. I was right in front of him, inches from his face. Before I could move, he leaned forward and kissed me quickly. It was a light kiss, no tongue, a quick peck really, as if it was a sudden impulse, a quick test of our feelings for each other.

He pulled back. "I, um—"

I felt like he was about to apologize and that was the last thing I wanted. "It's okay," I said. What I should have said was that it was good. All good. Chris Kern had just kissed me. Me—Hannah.

"What about Nick?" Chris said. "You two—"

"No," I rushed to say. "Zoe tried to set me up with him and he thought I liked him but I didn't. I mean, I don't. I never did and there's nothing between us." I sounded young again and I worried Chris would change his mind about wanting to kiss me.

"At the restaurant it seemed like—"

I cut him off. "I know what it seemed like and it's not."

"That's why I canceled this morning," he admitted. "Not because of it being grand prix day."

"I wondered," I said.

It felt like we both were trying to think of what to say to each other. It felt like there was more that needed to be said, but neither of us knew how yet. It was probably good I didn't say anything more because my mind was going crazy with endorphins. Chris had kissed me! *He* had kissed *me*! It was like everything I'd wanted since the very first day of Circuit was coming true.

# Chapter 21

CHRIS AND I RESUMED OUR lessons Sunday morning. I jumped an exercise Chris had set up and I actually rode it well. Logan was going better too. At the end of the lesson, Chris said he'd text me later. Neither one of us mentioned the kiss, but something had clearly changed between us.

In the ring that day, I had two rails but it was the best eight-fault course I had ever had. Logan was listening to me and we were finding distances to most of the jumps. Chris texted me after the class and I texted back asking if he was going to Backcountry because Zoe wanted me to go with her. He said he'd go if I went and after a few more back-and-forths we had made a plan to go together. He would pick me up.

At Backcountry, Chris told me more about what it was like riding for Harris. Harris didn't see the horses like Chris saw them. He didn't see them as animals and athletes, but as high-powered machines whose parts could be fixed if they broke or who could be replaced all together. He didn't have a background in horses and didn't understand that it took a super long time and a lot of patience to bring along a grand prix horse. Chris told me that his best horse, Nova, was hurt because Harris had insisted Chris keep showing him even when Chris was convinced something didn't feel quite right. Now that horse was out for the year, maybe forever, and Chris was off the European tour because none of his other horses were experienced enough yet. Nova had been his one big international horse.

"Buddy could be really good. I mean he's got the scope and the heart, but he's only seven. He needs another year doing the small grand prix classes and the 1.40 meter classes and taking it slow. I don't want to push it and ruin him."

"That's why you didn't do the inside turn?"

"There were only seven in the jump-off. A slower clean was still going to get a good piece of the action. Maybe at the end of the circuit I'll push him more than I did, but there was no reason to do that. I was still second for heaven's sake."

Chris drank his beer. Tommy Kinsler came over and chatted with him. Chris introduced me to him and Tommy shook my hand. A few weeks ago I was some nobody and now here I was at a bar with Chris Kern, meeting other grand prix riders. It still blew my mind. And what blew my mind even more was how comfortable I felt with Chris.

After Tommy left, I asked Chris how he'd come to work for Harris. Chris explained how Harris's company had sponsored a grand prix in Florida and Harris had become enthralled by the horses. He'd been enticed by the fact that you could be somebody in the sport without riding yourself. And it wasn't like other sports where you had to be a billionaire to own a professional team and even then, it was nearly impossible to become even a part owner of a team. Racehorses were equally expensive and exclusive. But show jumping was more of an open door. He'd bought one horse for Terry Hyde, the grand prix rider Chris had worked for when he'd started out as a professional. The horse did pretty well, placing in some grand prix classes. Harris got a taste of winning, of being the big shot who showed up to watch his horse. And he wanted more. Terry had other clients and Harris wanted his own trainer. He and Chris became friends and Harris saw Chris's talent. That was one thing Chris appreciated him for.

"I thought it'd be perfect. He offered to support me and buy me horses. He said he'd let me choose the horses and basically do all the training. But then the more he watched, the more he thought he knew. What do they say, a little power can be a dangerous thing? Well, now he thinks he knows everything."

Chris sipped his beer. "But I'm stuck with him. If I lose the ride on his horses I've got nothing."

"Could you teach? You're so good."

"Yeah, I could start my own training barn, but that takes a ton of time and energy, not to mention money, and then what, I have to hope I get some clients who want to buy a grand prix horse? Maybe I put together a syndicate." Chris looked out over the bar. "I don't mean to sound lazy. I mean Tommy, Anders, a lot of people have done it that way. But then there are the riders with their own money or their parents' money and they never have to think about how to afford the horses. I just thought I had such a good thing going. It could take a long while to get back to having the right horses."

I had never thought much about who owned the horses in the grand prix classes and how hard it was to find sponsors. Or what it meant to deal with a sponsor. Chris was such a great rider and a great horseman and it was wonderful how much he cared about his horses. That seemed like it should be enough to guarantee someone success, but it wasn't.

I saw Zoe come into the room. She had her hair down and was wearing a short skirt and tight top. She looked super pretty, but she also looked like she was on the prowl. I had seen Dermott over at the bar earlier and I hoped that what Zoe said was true—that this time she was really done with him.

She came over to our table and plopped herself right down on my lap. I smelled alcohol on her breath—she'd been pre-gaming, of course.

"Hey there, Chiquita banana!" she said.

"Chiquita banana?" I said.

She giggled. "I don't know. It just popped into my head. What are you two doing? Just hanging out? Chris, you rocked it yesterday. Second place—nice!"

"Thanks," he said.

Zoe moved off my lap into a chair and told us the latest gossip about Eve's horse that won the grand prix about to be sold to a junior rider. "That's what you need to win in the juniors these days," Zoe said. "A grand prix horse."

Zoe went to get a drink from the bar. I leaned closer to Chris. "Dermott's up there."

"Oh no," he said.

"Yup."

Chris sighed. "Zoe, Zoe, Zoe."

I watched Zoe take in the sight of Dermott. He was talking with two girls I didn't know but kind of recognized. Now that I'd been at show for a few weeks there were a lot of people I knew by face, if still not by name. She ordered and I could tell she was pretending not to care about Dermott. When she came back from the bar, she had a drink and Mike with her. "Look who I found!"

Mike seemed a little uncomfortable as he sat down next to us, but Chris was super nice and introduced himself right away. During the day the line between grooms and riders was clearer; at nights it could get fuzzy. I noticed Zoe inching closer to Mike and holding his gaze longer than usual. Zoe got up to go to the bathroom and when she came back Mike watched her walk all the way to the table with this goofy love-struck look.

Zoe flirted more with him, at one point challenging him to a contest where you have to make the other person smile. Mike was pretty good at not smiling and the rules were you weren't supposed to touch each other, but Zoe managed to somehow straddle his chair and get as close as possible to him without touching him before he smiled and she fell into his lap. I got excited watching them, thinking that finally Zoe was liking someone who liked her back and was a good guy. Mike would be nice to her. Mike would take care of her. Mike would be good for her.

The next time she had to go to the bathroom Zoe dragged

me with her. She put on lipstick and told me to borrow hers when I was done.

"This is so good—you and Mike," I said, looking at her in the mirror.

"I know I'm totally flirting with him, right?"

"He's so into you."

Zoe gave me a dismissive wave. "Whatever. I'm just trying to make Dermott jealous. I swear he looked over when I fell on to Mike's lap. Did you see him? Was he looking at me?"

I put the lipstick cap on, feeling sick to my stomach. "You're just pretending?"

Zoe put her hands on her hips. "I told you I'd never be interested in Mike. He's a groom."

I thought of the way Mike was looking at her. "You can't do that to him. That's so cruel."

Zoe made a face. "He's a big boy. He'll live." She pressed her lips together and I gave her back the lipstick.

At the table, I couldn't even look at Mike. He'd been so nice to me. He'd helped me out so many times already. He didn't deserve this kind of treatment. Chris must have noticed that I didn't seem right because he gave me a concerned look. Zoe said she was going to get another drink. Mike offered to get it for her, but Zoe insisted she go. At the bar, she elbowed her way in next to Dermott to order. Her drink came and she stayed there, talking to him. He seemed interested in her now—her gross plan must have worked.

Mike saw them too and his face drained of color. I didn't know what to say to him. Should I have been telling him she'd never been interested in him? That seemed cruel too. Finally, when she still hadn't come back, I said, "I don't know why she has a weakness for that guy. He's so awful."

Mike's face looked pained. "I think I'm going to call it a night."

"Mike—" I said as he stood up. "Wait—" But what else was there to say or do?

Dermott now had his hand across Zoe's back, like they were a couple.

"She doesn't know what's good for her," I said.

Mike nodded. "Yeah, I know. But I can't stay and watch that . . ." He gave her one more look and turned to leave.

"I think I want to go too," I said to Chris a few moments later. Zoe and Dermott were nearly intertwined and it was clear where this was heading. Again. "I can't believe she could be so stupid. She's not really doing this again, is she?"

"I know," Chris said. "She's not in good shape. She's one of those rider orphans who's so messed up."

"Rider orphan?"

"Raised on the circuit by trainers. Her parents don't care about her. I feel sorry for her."

"Well, I feel pissed at her. She said in the bathroom she was just using Mike to make Dermott jealous."

"Let's go." Chris stood up and I followed him.

In the car, I went on a tirade of how mad I was at Zoe and how horrible she was for doing that to sweet Mike.

Chris said, "Mike'll be okay."

We parked outside of my condo.

"But it's just not fair. It's not fair to Mike, and Dermott

should be gelded or something. And Zoe should just know better. And Harris should realize what a great rider you are and that he can't afford to lose you."

I banged my fist on my thigh. It was like letting my anger out at Zoe made all my feelings come rushing out. Chris smiled at me. "Easy, easy. You're freaking out here." He placed his hand on mine on my thigh, making me realize that it wasn't just all those feelings about Zoe and Mike and Dermott that were bubbling over, but how I felt about Chris. I wanted him in a way I hadn't ever wanted anyone before. He must have sensed it because the next thing I knew we were kissing madly. Not lightly kissing but pressing our faces and our mouths together, full of feelings we'd kept inside. We went on like that for minutes, making out with a fierce intensity. Finally, tired, red-faced, lips nearly sore, we pulled apart.

"Well," Chris said.

"Yeah," I replied. It was a relief to kiss him like that. To let my pent-up feelings for him out. Apparently he'd been holding them in too.

"I think we steamed up the windows." Chris wiped away the fog with his hand.

"That was—" I began.

"Good," he said. "Very good and very overdue."

# Chapter 22

CHRIS DIDN'T COME IN that night. I didn't know if Cheryl was there, not that she would have cared if I brought Chris inside (it might have set off a wildfire of horse show gossip), but I didn't offer and he didn't ask. It seemed like we were both okay taking things a little slowly as we tried to figure out what our feelings about each other meant. I couldn't help but think how Chris was a grand prix rider whose life revolved around the show circuit and I was just here for a few more weeks before heading to college. Zoe would have said not to think about the future, but that wasn't like me. I didn't tell her about Chris because I felt funny about it. For one thing, we didn't know what "it" was that was going on between us, and what if he didn't want me to tell her?

Monday was super hot and humid, up into the nineties, and Zoe got a group together to go to the quarry. Hundreds of years ago, Weathersville became home to the country's first marble quarry. As demand for the marble grew, several other quarries were built in the area. Now defunct, the leftover quarries were still stunning with their huge, gleaming slabs of marble. There were hidden quarries that you had to walk on old, overgrown mining trails to get to, but the quarry Zoe meant was off one of the main roads.

She must have invited Chris because he pulled in a few minutes after Zoe, Jed, and I did. I wondered if he'd come mainly because of me, or if that was hoping for too much. Maybe he and Zoe hung out on off-days?

Zoe wore a tiny, orange string bikini and she looked amazing in it. I had a bikini on too, but mine wasn't as skimpy. Still, I felt Chris's eyes on me when I pulled my shirt over my head.

All of us had terrible farmer's tans, even Zoe. It was as if we had white polo shirts painted on and white socks that ran all the way up to our upper thighs. We stuck out among all the local kids who spent more than one day all summer in a bathing suit.

Chris had a farmer's tan too, but it didn't make him any less gorgeous. His chest was totally drool-inducing. He had a six-pack and strong, muscular upper arms. I wondered whether he worked out in addition to riding. Probably.

Chris suggested we jump from the rocks high up in the quarry. He assured us it was plenty deep. We had seen a few other kids do it. It wasn't crazy high, but it was higher than a regular town pool diving board. Zoe didn't want to. She shimmied into the water from the low marble slabs instead. It was me who followed Chris and jumped off after him without even second-guessing it. It wasn't Zoe, who rode in the junior jumpers, slept with foreign men who were good in bed, and wore the orange bikini. It was me, and that surprised and thrilled me. I seemed to keep finding out things about myself that I had never known before.

That night Zoe suggested we drive an hour to see a local rodeo. I had never been to a rodeo and of course I was happy to do anything that included Chris. Jed couldn't go so it was just the three of us. Chris offered to drive and Zoe sat up front. She had a can of Arizona iced tea that she sipped out of occasionally. What I didn't know, but would find out from her later, was that the can was a mix of iced tea and vodka. Zoe turned the radio onto a country station and she sang along to the songs she knew, which were a lot of them. It made me realize she was a real southern girl, born and bred. Finally a song came on that I knew by heart—MISSION, by Low Flying Planes. It was kind of a combo between country and pop and it was getting a lot of airtime on both stations. It was about a guy making it his mission to get this girl to fall in love with him. Zoe turned it up and belted out the lyrics.

The first half hour of driving was on the highway, but then we drove on smaller and smaller roads until we bumped along on a dirt road for several miles. I would never have believed we were going the right way if it weren't for the other cars kicking up dust in front and behind us.

Finally we passed a shed-row stable and parked alongside hundreds of other pick-up trucks and cars in a huge grass field. The rodeo ring was small but well lit with metal bleachers around it like the kind you find at high school baseball games. There was one food stand offering corn dogs, fried dough, hot dogs, and sodas, with a huge line of people waiting. There were families, older people, and girls in tight jeans, tighter shirts, and cowboy boots, and guys in cowboy hats. It was a world away from the horse show scene and I felt like we had been dropped into another life.

We sat down in the stands and Zoe struck up a flirtatious conversation with two cowboys. One was cuter than the other, with blue eyes and blond hair and a goatee. She got them to explain all about the different events. I knew how annoying horse show people found it when they had to try to explain the hunters and the jumpers and the eq, but these two guys didn't seem to mind, probably because they hoped it might lead somewhere with Zoe.

The cute cowboy offered to get beers from his truck and Zoe jumped up and followed him. She had finished the vodka in her iced tea can on the way.

"Oh God," I said to Chris. "Here we go again."

He smiled at me like I was being a little dramatic. Even though he'd known Zoe for much longer than I had, I felt like I knew her better than he did. I could see just where this was going. How could Chris not see what I was seeing?

The line for food had dwindled and Chris decided to buy us fried dough. I sat there the whole time he was gone, hoping Zoe would come back. But when Chris climbed the risers carrying a paper plate with fried dough that smelled amazing, she hadn't returned. The friend of the cute cowboy had told me he was going to go see what was taking them so long, but I had watched him and he'd just gone across the ring and sat with some other friends so clearly checking on them was a big fat lie.

Chris broke off a piece of the fried dough and handed it to me. It tasted so good, especially the slightly damp confectioners sugar on top, that for a few moments I stopped thinking about Zoe. I also let myself bask in the fact that I was at a rodeo with Chris Kern. Would something happen between us tonight to finally make this undeniably real? But by the time the dough was almost all the way gone, I checked the stands across the ring and saw the friend of the cute cowboy laughing with his other buddies. That brought me straight back to Zoe.

"We have to go find her," I said. "Make sure she's okay." I was having terrible thoughts of her getting raped by the cute cowboy. His friend knew better than to go check on him—he knew just what was going on. Zoe was flirting with the guy, but she didn't actually want to hook up with some total stranger at a rodeo, did she?

Chris didn't argue with me. Maybe he was thinking some of the same stuff I was thinking, imagining the worst.

The field was lined with cars now. And it was dark.

"I don't know how we'll ever find her," I said as we got to the first row of cars.

"I guess we call her name," Chris said. He cupped his hand to his mouth. "Zoe?"

We walked through the lines of cars just like that, calling her name. I started walking faster and then I was nearly running, imagining her in my mind trying to push the guy off her. I'd gotten farther away from Chris and then I heard him say, "Hannah, over here."

I ran over, my heart beating, just waiting to find disaster.

What I found was Chris with his hands on his hips giving me a look that said, "Glad we were so worried."

And there was Zoe, with the guy's cowboy hat on her head, wiping her mouth with the back of her hand. The first few buttons of her shirt were undone and the cute cowboy was doing up his shiny belt buckle. I had the distinct feeling Chris had found him with his jeans down around his cowboy boots and Zoe kneeling in front of him. I couldn't understand what she would want to do that for. Why would she want to blow some random guy in a rodeo parking lot? Didn't she think better of herself than that? And for that matter, what had Chris thought of seeing Zoe and him?

"Zoe," I said. "We're leaving."

"I can give her a ride home," the cute cowboy said.

"No," Chris said.

It took Zoe a few pouty faces until she walked away from him. She scowled once more at us, acting like we were parents ruining all her fun. She took off his hat and tossed it back to him.

In the car driving out the dirt driveway, she was giggling. "I've always wanted to mess around with a cowboy."

"I don't even think he was a real cowboy," I said. "The real ones were riding."

"Cowboy enough for me," she said.

The ride home didn't feel as long as the ride there. Maybe it was because the small, dirt roads came first this time and then we were on the highway.

Chris had to drop me off first—my condo was before Zoe's and it would have been weird to go past my house to hers. I thought of saying I'd keep him company, but decided not to. Right before I got out of the car, Chris and I locked gazes and it was as if we were both wanting the same thing and couldn't say it.

"Bye, now," Zoe said, in a heavy cowgirl accent, oblivious about interrupting our moment. "Y'all take care!"

"Bye," I said.

Chris waited till I was inside to pull away.

In bed, later, I wanted to text him so badly. And I prayed he would text me, but the only texts I got were from Zoe about the cute cowboy. The texts started out saying how good a kisser he was and got more rapid and explicit as the night went on, saying what she wanted to do to him.

*Aren't you going to go to sleep?* I finally wrote at 1:30.

*Nah, wired. Can't sleep. Probably gonna stay up all nite.*

*Go to bed!*

*Yes, Mom.*

*Now!*

*You're no fun.*

*Turning off my phone,* I wrote back.

*Lame-o.*

*Yeah, I know.*

# Chapter 23

CHRIS TAUGHT ME ON TUESDAY like usual. We were jumping every other day now, but he still kept focusing on fundamentals like gymnastics and getting my eye working. He set up a broken line with low jumps set on the half-stride and made me do it leaving out the stride and then adding the stride over and over again until I got it right.

On Wednesday I was back showing again. I did the 1.00 meter class at the beginning of the week and then the children's on Friday, Saturday, and Sunday. I had definitely improved, but that didn't always translate into doing particularly well in the ring. Typically, I still had a stop every now and then, and I nearly always had at least one rail. But some things had gotten better. Logan wasn't running away with me anymore and the stops I had were because I asked for a terrible distance.

In the schooling ring, Jamie called to me occasionally as she did five other things including text and talk to another trainer. "Get the oxer one more time," she said. "Don't pull to nothing this time, Hannah."

Okay, so I wasn't supposed to pull to nothing. But what was I supposed to be doing so I didn't end up pulling to nothing? I decided whatever I did, this time I wouldn't pull.

I came around the corner and did not take back on the reins. We caught a major flyer and nearly ran into another rider after the jump when I could barely turn Logan.

"Okay, you didn't pull, but you also didn't make a choice either."

I didn't make a choice. What the hell did that mean? All Jamie did was utterly confuse me. I pulled Logan up and asked very gingerly, "Um, what should I have done there?" I wasn't being impertinent. I literally wanted to know what I should be doing. But in Jamie's world, riders were supposed to do, not ask.

"What do you think you were supposed to do? Find a distance and then ride it! Is that really that hard for you? Try it again."

Well, that cleared it all up. This time I pulled a little, and somehow we didn't completely chip. Jamie said it was good enough and I was ready to go in the ring.

It was like in my lessons with Chris, everything about riding became clear and made sense. I think I relaxed because I knew he cared about me and actually knew what he was doing. And therefore Logan relaxed. Then everything changed when Jamie was helping me and I went back to my old bad-riding self.

At the in-gate, I told myself to forget about Jamie. To try to ride like Chris was watching me, which he usually was if he could. I scanned the outside of the ring. Yup, there he was on Buddy at the far corner of the ring.

I took a deep breath and when it was my turn, walked calmly into the ring, trying to channel Chris. The tone sounded and I pressed Logan into a canter. The first jump was an inviting ramp oxer with blue and yellow rails. It was funny how the color of the rails could make a jump inviting or not. I personally did not like red or black rails. Yellow and blue were my favorites. Green, pink, and purple were okay. Chris said Logan loved to jump and at first I had thought he was crazy because Logan had refused so many times with me. But I had come to realize he was right. Logan always pricked up his ears and he wanted at that jump badly. It was just that sometimes I messed him up so much when we got there.

I turned to the oxer. Thankfully it was a short approach off the rail so Logan didn't have time to build. A good, normal distance was there and we were over fence one and headed to two, three, and four—a line across the diagonal. Logan raced a little to two and we were deep, but it was a vertical and he managed to clear it. The jump height wasn't the problem for him. The rails were always rider-error. I lost count of the strides to fence three. I was supposed to do five strides and I hoped that was what I did. I made sure to count to fence four—I did the six strides I was supposed to do there. I turned to the in-and-out on the short side of the ring. It was up next to the spectator tent and had box walls underneath it that made it spooky. Logan sucked back a little and then burst forward—his version of a spook. We chipped the in, but made it out okay. All in all this was going pretty darn well.

Fence six was a rainbow swoop skinny. We were long to it and then on the other side I had to pull pretty hard to slow Logan down. Somehow we managed to get over fence seven, a square lime-green oxer. Then it was on to the last line—a vertical to a triple combination. It was headed toward the in-gate and I was fighting to slow Logan down nearly all the way around the corner. I tried to let go a little so I wouldn't pull to nothing, if that was even what I was doing, and the vertical was fine. It was six strides to the triple. When we had walked it, Jamie said the steady six strides was a definite maybe. I was counting out loud, one, two, three. Oh no, it was becoming clear to me that six was not ever going to happen at this rate. Stride four I did nothing—kind of like I was in a state of shock, frozen. Stride five I made a lame attempt at steadying Logan, but it was too late. He left out the stride and we flew into the triple. I braced myself for rails to clatter and maybe for Logan to crash. I said, "whoa" out loud, a pathetic at-tempt at saving our lives. Somehow Logan managed to pop through the triple, picking his knees up, and not coming close to touching the rails of the first two jumps. I was so surprised I fell behind him on the last effort and caught him in the mouth. He dragged his back toes and had the rail of the last oxer down. Rider-error again.

"And the last jump unfortunately comes down for four faults," the announcer said as I circled Logan.

I breathed a sigh of relief. I learned the jump-off every time, but I think I would have fainted if I had to do it. Would I even remember it? Maybe. Let's just say four faults was fine with me. I wondered if somehow Logan had even pulled the rail on purpose. It was a ridiculous thought but I felt like the look on his face said, "Don't worry, I know you're not ready for that. Maybe soon."

Jamie was waiting for me as I came out of the ring. "Better," she said. She gave me a funny look, like she was trying to figure out how the hell I pulled off a round that was one step above my usual tragic and treacherous.

"Thanks," I said.

I think I must have stunned her into silence because she just said once more, "Better."

# Chapter 24

CHRIS TEXTED ME: *pretty good ride.*

I wrote back: *i know, right?!*

That week we started texting a lot. We would keep in touch about what we were both doing. What he was doing was always more exciting than what I was doing. I would be cleaning Logan's stall or giving him a bath while Chris was schooling a horse or riding in a class. When I could, I always watched him show. I loved watching him. I got to know his horses and what they went like. I knew what was hard for them and what Chris was working on with them. I liked the horse that Chris had thought was special, Arkos, but Chris wasn't exaggerating—he always had at least one rail down, even when it looked like Chris rode it perfectly. It drove Chris crazy. He had done everything to figure out what might be bothering the horse. He'd checked for ulcers and sores in his mouth. He'd tried acupuncture, massage, a new saddle that was custom designed for his back, an ergonomic girth, un-conventional bits, therapeutic saddle pads, even a full body bone scan—you name it, he had tried it. The only thing he hadn't tried yet was a psychic.

"You could try it, why not?" I said, when I was at Chris's barn after yet another four-fault performance by Arkos. There was one particular psychic, Ann, whom tons of horse show people used. "Zoe swears by it. Her mother had a horse that was lame and they couldn't figure out why and the psychic said it was because his blankets didn't fit right. They got different blankets and he was sound the next day. I mean, how would she know that?"

Chris shrugged. "I don't know. I'm just not sure I'm so desperate I'm going to go the psychic route." Chris went to work on the dry-erase chart that outlined what each horse would do each day. "Do you want to go out to dinner tonight?" he asked.

"Like just you and me?" I said.

"Ah, yeah, that's what I was thinking."

"Sure," I said.

I had wondered if Chris was embarrassed about being seen with me, but if he wanted to have dinner alone with me, he had to be okay with it. Did that mean I could tell Zoe about our make-out session?

"I know a great place. It's a little farther from here, but you'll love it. I'll pick you up at seven."

A little farther from here. Did that mean just the opposite—that he didn't want to be seen with me? Why wouldn't we go to one of the places around here? Oh well. I tried not to care. Chris had asked me out to dinner and that was what I would focus on.

* * *

The place Chris took me to looked like a rustic cabin from the outside. And it didn't have amazing décor in the inside either—plain, chunky wooden tables covered in old school red checkered vinyl tablecloths and solid wooden chairs. But it was packed and we got the last table. The menu was simple too—spaghetti with a choice of sauces, ravioli, a house salad with homemade dressing they sold in mason jars at the front counter. The waitress brought us bread right after she handed us the menus.

"This is one of my favorite restaurants," Chris said.

I wanted to believe him, but I worried he was just trying to cover up the fact that he wasn't sure he wanted to be seen with me.

"How did you find this place?" I asked.

"Jimmy told me about it. His summer place is around here."

I assumed he meant grand prix rider, Jimmy Sharpe. I wasn't going to ask and seem dumb.

Chris offered me a piece of bread. "Do you like garlic bread? It's straight from the oven. The most amazing garlic bread I've ever eaten."

I took a piece and bit into it. Chris was right. It was delicious. But as I swallowed I wondered if we'd kiss tonight. I sure hoped so, but now my breath would smell like garlic. Of course, so would Chris's.

"I guess I should have asked if you liked Italian food," Chris said.

"Who doesn't like Italian?" I said.

"Only people on diets, I guess," Chris said. "My ex, she was always dieting."

Chris bit his lower lip, like he wished he hadn't said anything about his ex. I decided I would be all mature about it and not pretend I had no idea he had dated Mary Beth for years.

"That was Mary Beth McCord?" I said.

He nodded. "Yeah."

"And she's in Europe with the Developing Riders Team?"

"Yeah."

"She was always dieting?"

"She was skinny, she just was a little obsessed with the way she looked. She stayed away from carbs."

I took another big bite of bread as if to make a statement.

"I ended up never cooking for her because no matter what I made it had too many carbs," he said.

"You cook?" I said, surprised.

"I can do things other than ride a horse," he said.

"Like cook." I couldn't imagine any of the guys in my high school cooking. It made Chris seem so much older and more mature. Oh yeah, and totally sexy. You wouldn't think something like cooking would make a guy seem sexy, but it made him seem self-sufficient and competent.

"Like cook. And I can ski. I've been known to crack a book every so often."

"How'd you learn to cook?"

"Dale taught me. Going out every night can get old. I can't really cook complicated stuff—just a few healthy meals."

"You and Dale seem really close."

Chris nodded. "He's family. He's been there for me through everything and anything. There's no one I trust more in the world."

I remembered the way Dale had looked at me—like I was a distraction Chris didn't need. Getting close to Chris would seem like it would involve Dale approving of you. I wondered how Dale had felt about Mary Beth.

I asked about what it had been like growing up on the show circuit. Chris said he hadn't completely. "I played soccer and baseball when I was a kid. I didn't get serious about horses till I was fourteen or fifteen so it wasn't like I've only ever done this."

"How did you know you wanted to only ride?"

"It just got more and more fun, and intense. I love the horses, the competition. I can't imagine doing anything else, even on my worst days."

"So you knew what you wanted to do since you were like sixteen?"

"Pretty much."

"That's really cool. I have no idea what I want to do."

"You don't have to. You'll figure it out."

The rest of the meal was just like the garlic bread—simple but unbelievable. I began to wonder if Chris wasn't trying to take me somewhere that no one would see us, but instead take me someplace he liked.

The whole drive back to Weathersville felt charged. We talked some, but I had this feeling that we both wanted to get back and see what would happen next. I kept thinking about our make-out session in the car. Would we make it inside this time? It took too long to get back. The roads were dark and Chris had to go slow. Once we saw three deer on the side of the road. As we were nearing the show, Chris said, "So do you want to go back to your condo, or would you want to come over to mine for a while?"

"I'll go to yours," I said. I was surprised at how easily those words came out of my mouth. It was like how I'd jumped off the rocks at the quarry. I was nervous about what would happen, and whether I was terribly inexperienced in an embarrassing way. But something about Chris and his assured nature made me think everything would be okay.

Finally, we pulled into the driveway, the gravel crunching under the tires.

Jasper greeted us, wagging his tail and nuzzling Chris. Chris let him outside. I'd learned that Jasper was a rescue. He looked like a German Shepherd, only all white. He adored Chris and was crazy attached to him—always sitting right by him whenever Chris was around. We watched in the light of the porch as Jasper ran to a tree, lifted his leg, and then ran back.

"Good dog," Chris said.

We walked into the kitchen. I looked around, unsure of what came next. How did this go from here? I tried to think of something to say to make the moment less awkward. What was I supposed to do? Then, Chris stepped close to me. Any awkwardness between us evaporated as I looked into his eyes. He knew what he wanted and how to go about it. That's how it happened. One of us knew what he was doing.

With assured movements he kissed me, and it was easy to

follow his lead. Soon it was just like in the car, both of us hungry for each other. He ran his hand up my back, under my shirt, and then around to the front over my bra.

He took me to the couch in the living room and peeled my shirt off over my head. Chris pulled my bra-straps down over my shoulders. Was this it, I wondered? Was I going to have sex with him tonight? Was I ready for that? This was Chris Kern. What girl wouldn't want her first time to be with him?

As he kissed my neck, I said, "Was that you, the night we all went out to dinner? Did you come by the horse show when I was checking on Logan?"

"Yes, that was me." He put his lips to my skin again and then said, "Are you weirded out, like I was stalking you or something?"

"No."

"I liked you and I wanted to see what was up with you and Nick. I also wanted to make sure you were okay."

Soon my bra was off. Chris took off his shirt. This was getting more than real. I placed my hands on his chest, like I'd thought about doing when he'd been shirtless at the quarry. He undid my jeans and with my help, shimmied them down my legs.

"Just one thing," I said.

"Yeah," he breathed into my ear.

"I'm not sure I want to have sex yet. I'm, well, I haven't before."

"Okay," he said. It didn't seem to upset or deter him. He said in a forced breath in my ear again, "Do you want to stop?"

"No," I said.

He reached for my hand and put it against his crotch. Through his jeans, I could feel his hard-on. "Neither do I," he said.

I undid his jeans and moved my hand first over his boxers and then under. It felt unexpectedly powerful to feel his dick, all firm and strong. I liked it more than I ever imagined I might. And it was hard for *me*. I had made him this way. As I held him in my hand, his breathing quickened. I could feel the want in him and it thrilled me that it was all because of me. The word 'cock' ran through my head—I had never really thought of a penis as anything but a hard-on or a dick, but Chris's hard-on was so big in my hand, so firm, the word cock seemed right to describe it. I liked holding him in my hand. I liked the feel of him. But at the same time, I couldn't quite imagine him being inside me. That seemed like it would hurt.

He moaned as I kept touching him, moving my hand up and down. I guess I was doing something right. Soon he moved his hand down. He started out touching me lightly over my panties. It felt good, but I almost had a hard time concentrating on him and myself at the same time. He slid his hand under my panties and it started to feel really good, and I concentrated less on what I was doing to him. It didn't seem to make much of a difference as his breathing was quickening. A hand-job. The word ran through my mind. That's what I was doing. I was giving him a hand-job. The few times I'd heard the expression it had seemed so industrial and emotionless. This was totally different. He pulled down my underwear and I held him a little tighter. A few moments later he groaned and I felt a spurt of liquid on my upper thigh. He took a breath, blew it out, and took his hand off of me. I missed his hand, but I knew it was over for him. I didn't quite know what to do about the mess on my leg, but Chris stood up, pulled up his jeans and went to the kitchen. He came back with paper towels and dried me off. "Sorry," he said.

"It's okay," I said, as I took in the sight of him in his jeans with no shirt.

It was all very okay.

# Chapter 25

AFTER THAT NIGHT, Chris and I fooled around whenever we could. It seemed like all both of us ever thought about was riding and hooking up. I spent every night at his house, on the couch, giving him hand-jobs and moving on from that to having him rub up against me until he came. He always came and I felt proud that I had made him come. He hadn't made me come yet, but I had been close a couple of times. It was funny how hooking up came naturally. Here I was having only messed around with one guy before and within a week I was doing things I'd only imagined. I learned how to give Chris a blow job and it turned out to be something I didn't really need to learn. I went down there and opened my mouth and the rest all came rather naturally. It made me think again of birds. No one told them how to do a mating dance or how to mate. They knew how in their DNA. It felt kind of the same for me. Maybe it helped that Chris had surely done it all before and so he wasn't awkward about any of it. He also wasn't shy about signaling what felt good with a moan or an "oh yeah" so I learned quickly when I was doing it right. I went back home every night—I guess so Cheryl didn't get suspicious although I didn't think she really would have cared. But that was all I needed—somehow it getting back to my mother that I wasn't coming home some nights.

We continued with our morning lessons at the show and Logan kept getting better. My eye was getting better too. At the show, Chris and I hung out some and texted all the time. I'd go by his barn or we'd sit by the ring together sometimes. Often it was with Jed or Zoe. Chris was busy during the days, so I'm not sure anyone really suspected what was going on between us. Zoe and Jed surely didn't, or else I know they would have said something. Unfortunately, Zoe had a new guy in mind for me—Teddy. He was an amateur, only one year out of the juniors, and showed in the jumpers. He went to Trinity College, horse-showed in the summer, and flew back and forth to Florida to compete in the winters. I knew it wouldn't be long before I had to tell her about Chris. What I didn't know was that I wouldn't get the chance to tell her the right way.

\* \* \*

On Monday, Zoe arranged for us to go to Bromley. Zoe, Jed, me, and Teddy. Although I didn't want a repeat of the awkward dinner with Chris and Nick, I wished Chris was coming. But he had to drive to New York to look at a horse that a horse-dealer friend of his had gotten in from Europe. Chris was constantly checking out horses on Bigeq and other sites, and watching streaming of classes all over the country and world. He said it was hard to find a grand prix horse or even a young horse with potential to be a first horse because in the digital age when a horse had talent, everyone knew about it fast. So he felt he had to work extra hard to be the first to find out about a promising horse.

I hated going to Bromley without him and I wished I'd been able to road trip to look at the horse with him. I hadn't asked—it hadn't really occurred to me then, but now I could imagine us driving together, stopping for coffee along the way. It would have been fun to see the horse go, and watch Chris in action. But he probably wouldn't want me going with him. Who would he say I was, without rumors being started?

So I was going to Bromley, knowing that Zoe had told Teddy all about me.

Teddy was good-looking in a strong-jawed, toothy Kennedy-esque kind of way—I had to give Zoe that. He was well-dressed and ultra-confident. He and Zoe both had water bottles with them and when we were waiting in line for our tickets to ride the alpine slides, they clinked water bottles, which I realized meant that the bottles didn't have water in them. Zoe managed it so Teddy and I rode the chair lift up the mountain together. Teddy offered me a sip from his water bottle, which he explained was really vodka, and I said no thanks. His phone rang. He took the call and talked loudly, like what he was saying was supposed to impress me.

"Hey, man. Yeah, totally. Of course I'm going. It's a 100K class."

His talk continued—when he was getting to the horse show, plans for drinks and dinner. He finally hung up and said to me, "That was McNair Sutter."

I nodded. McNair Sutter was another young, amateur

grand prix rider. Somehow in this instance it was maybe worse that Teddy used McNair's full name—like he was making sure his name-dropping had its full effect.

"I'm going up to HITS next weekend on Sunday to ride in the big class there, then coming back," he explained.

I could maybe understand why grand prix riders like Chris, who were professionals and made their living off their results, show-hopped for the prize money, but it didn't really make sense for someone like Teddy or McNair, who didn't need the winnings to survive financially.

We got off the chair lift, but not until I had to endure Teddy's stories of heli-skiing in Alaska. I had never done alpine slides before. They were fun, but I didn't like going super fast. Of course, Teddy and Zoe did—especially fueled by vodka. The second time down they raced each other and Zoe went all out to beat Teddy. She lost control around one of the turns and tore up her elbows and knees on the cement track.

Somehow she was laughing—maybe she was so drunk it didn't hurt.

We stayed and had lunch and the whole time I had half my mind on Chris. Sometimes I'd think of the things we'd done together and my stomach would get all crazy-feeling. Teddy kept telling stories that seemed like he was a giant snob—how he'd sat in the front-row at the Jason Aldean concert, how he'd gone to the Super Bowl in Miami, and how he'd been to Macchu Picchu. Maybe he was trying too hard to impress me and it wasn't the real him, but it didn't matter. I felt zero attraction to him.

On the drive home, Zoe said, "Let me guess, you don't like him either?"

"He's pretty arrogant, don't you think?"

Zoe let out a frustrated sigh. "He's got money. Piles of it. Is that so bad?"

"Then why don't you go for him? Let me guess, too young?"

"I've known him forever. Like since we were doing ponies."

"He didn't seem interested in me either," I said.

"You didn't try very hard."

"What was I supposed to do?"

"Flirt with him! Drink a little! Loosen up!"

"I'm sorry," I said. "I think I'm hopeless. You should just give up on me."

"No way," Zoe said. "You and Teddy could still happen. We still have three weeks."

Three weeks. That was all I had left with Chris? How had the Circuit gone by so fast?

* * *

On Tuesday, Zoe was in a bad mood all day, sending me total downer texts. *My life sucks. This summer sucks.* She begged me to go out Tuesday night. *Who goes out Tues?* I texted her. *Just a few drinks*, she wrote back. *Okay*, I said. I guess I was still feeling badly about Teddy. I'd go out with her and then go over to Chris's.

I was surprised to find quite a few horse show people at Backcountry, including a bunch of young juniors, probably fourteen and fifteen, who managed to sneak in and were having the time of their lives. A couple of the young grand prix riders were buying them too many drinks and the girls were flirting outrageously with them. Here I still hadn't lost my virginity and they probably already had, or would by tomorrow morning. They were the next Zoe Tramell in the making.

And as for Zoe, it wasn't pretty. Dermott wasn't there and Zoe was pounding drink after drink. Her arms were bandaged from the road rash she'd gotten at Bromley.

I texted Chris and he said he was coming over. He showed up when Zoe was at the bar ordering another drink.

When Zoe came back to the table, she saw Chris and brightened for the first time that day. "Chris! When did you get here?"

"Just now and we're leaving," he said.

"Leaving?" Zoe made a pouty face. "We haven't even danced yet. Chris, when's the last time you've been out on the dance floor?"

"Not really my thing," Chris said.

"Well, tonight that all changes." Zoe stood up and suggestively shaped her hands down her body, shimmying her hips.

Chris shook his head. "Not tonight. You've had too much to drink and you know it."

"Chris! You're being such a buzz-kill."

"That may be, but we're leaving." He stood up.

Zoe took a defiant sip of her drink and said like a petulant child, "Well, I'm not."

"You don't have a ride home," I pointed out.

She glanced over to the dance floor. "I can find a way home."

I was sure she could and that was the problem right there.

Zoe made a show of storming off toward the bar. Sitting with his friends was one of the sleaziest members of the jump crew, Trevor. He looked half-stoned most of the time and had the work ethic of a slug. He was just doing this to make some bucks for the summer, goof off, and get laid, and didn't care at all about the horses or horse shows. He was the perfect target because he wouldn't ask any questions or think twice when a pretty girl made a move at him.

Zoe wiggled in between Trevor and another jump crew burnout. A lot of the jump crew were South Americans. But sometimes white kids filled in the holes in the crew. It was the South Americans who typically worked hard and took pride in their jobs—the white kids were the slackers and they generally never lasted more than a season. Sometimes they got fired mid-circuit for showing up late, still drunk, or high, or for falling asleep when they should be shagging rails.

While Zoe came on to Trevor, Chris and I discussed what we were going to do.

"We can't just leave her here," I said.

"Right, no way," Chris agreed.

"So how do we get her out of here?"

Zoe had pulled Trevor onto the dance floor. She threw her arms around his neck and in a matter of moments his hands had migrated from her hips to her ass. I had never witnessed such a fast coupling and probably never would again. What had Zoe said to him? Had she told him it was his lucky night and he was going to take her home? Maybe she hadn't said anything—maybe her body language told the story.

When they started making out, right there on the dance floor, Chris stalked to where she was and pulled her off Trevor. I had followed a few steps behind.

"Zoe," Chris said. "We're your friends and we're taking you home. No argument. Let's go. Don't cause a problem— that's not the way you want this to go down with people watching."

If I had said the same words, Zoe would have ignored me. But she listened to Chris. Of course by "people" watching he meant the horse show people there who were addicted to gossip like other people were addicted to pain killers. Gossip was always best when it featured a top rider—and a junior, no less. Zoe was impeccable and unbeatable in the ring—and too many people would love nothing better than to see her screw up outside of the ring.

"What's the problem, man?" Trevor said to Chris. "She's having fun. I'll take good care of her."

That was just creepy. Chris didn't answer Trevor. With Chris on one side and me on the other, we walked Zoe, wobbling, to the door. Why had Zoe come to her senses? Maybe she knew what she was doing was a terrible idea and she just couldn't save herself, or maybe she was just beyond wasted?

I helped Zoe into the front seat of Chris's car and said I'd follow behind them.

"If you feel like you might throw up, tell me and I'll stop the car," Chris said to her before I closed the door.

"I feel fine," Zoe said, which was ridiculous because she was a total mess. Her face was red and blotchy and her always-pretty hair had gotten nearly knotted looking.

At Zoe's I parked behind Chris, got out, and opened Zoe's door. She didn't move right away.

"Can you walk?" I said. "Are you okay?"

"I'm just so mad at myself, you know? Why did I ever sleep with that DB Dermott? I feel so stupid."

Zoe was quiet for a few moments and then I heard her sniffle and she wiped her nose with her arm. She tried to wipe away her tears, but she couldn't stop crying. She was really sobbing now. "I'm so dumb."

"Hey, hey," Chris said in a kind voice. "You're not dumb. You're a smart girl who made a mistake. We all make mistakes."

Zoe looked at him. "Really? You don't think I'm some dumb slut?"

Again, it was like Chris's words meant everything to her. Did she only listen to guys?

Chris said, "No way. Why would I ever think that about you? The one who looks bad is Dermott."

Zoe smiled through her tears. "Thank you, Chris." She turned to look at me. "You guys are the best. I don't know what I'd do without you. I mean it. You guys are awesome."

"Are you going to be okay?" Chris asked.

Zoe nodded. "Yeah."

"Get some sleep. And before you go to bed drink a big glass of water and take two aspirin if you have them."

I wished I knew all these tricks of the trade, but bird

courtship was more my domain than hangover remedies. Chris knew the right things to say and what she should do. He was kind to her—maybe too kind, I was beginning to think. Maybe she needed a harsh wake-up call to change her life. It wasn't only Dermott's fault—it was Zoe's too.

I walked Zoe to the door, making sure she got in. Chris waited and I came over to talk to him through the car window. I said, "You were really nice to her."

"I think she kind of needs someone to be nice to her."

"Do you think though she maybe needs to face the truth? I mean, she is kind of acting like a dumb slut." The words felt rougher than I meant them to be. I followed up with, "I just don't want her to keep blaming guys like Dermott when she needs to value herself more, you know? It's not just Dermott. What about the guy from the rodeo?"

"It's a good point," Chris said. "I hadn't thought of it that way."

"Well, maybe that's the kind of thing that's better talked about when she's not drunk

and hysterical," I offered.

"So, what's up now?" Chris said.

"It's late," I said. It was after midnight.

"You're going home?"

I smiled. "I didn't say that."

"You could sleep over," Chris said.

I thought about it. Would Cheryl notice, or care that I didn't come home? Did I care? I wanted to be with Chris tonight.

"I'll follow you," I said, even though I knew the way.

We didn't agree that we would have sex that night, but somehow we both knew this was the night. That it was finally happening. We had fooled around many times and it shouldn't have felt that special. But it did. Was it because society made such a big deal about sexual intercourse, or because I could get pregnant if we weren't careful? Those might be questions for a Gender, Sexuality, and Society class I might take at Tufts. Right then, all I knew was that this night, this time, meant something more than all the rest.

As Chris pulled off his shirt and lay down next to me, he said, "Is this how you imagined it? Or did you want rose petals and mood lighting?"

My stomach seized up a little. I wasn't just imagining things. This was happening.

"I really wish my virginity wasn't so . . . out there," I said.

"Like you would have just pretended you'd done it before?"

"I don't know. Maybe." But I knew that wasn't the truth. If I'd pretended I wasn't a virgin, we'd have had sex by now. And it wouldn't have been the same. It would have felt false and hollow, lying to him, pretending to be someone I wasn't.

Chris was close to me, his breath on my face. He kissed my neck. "We don't have to, but I'd be lying if I said I didn't want you right now."

His words sent good shivers up my spine. We kissed again. The feeling of tightness in my stomach was still sort of there, but there was another feeling too, lower.

"I want to," I said.

He stood up and went to get a condom. Or at least that's

what I assumed he was doing. I sat up and watched him disappear into the bathroom. It reassured me to see his clothes on a chair in the corner of the room, a pair of breeches on the dresser. The closet door was open and I saw his show shirts and jackets. I can't explain why I liked seeing his clothes, but I did. I knew him. I knew who he was. This wasn't Zoe and the wanna-be cowboy.

He came back and I watched him slide the condom onto himself. I'd never in a million years thought seeing a guy put on a condom would be sexy but it was. It was really sexy.

There were other surprises too.

I thought it would hurt a lot, but it didn't. Maybe it was because of my riding, or maybe that was just another myth about first times. I didn't bleed either. It also didn't take as long as I thought it would. For a few moments it felt intense and pleasurable, but in a different kind of way, a deeper, inside way. He had most of the pleasure this time—groaning in my ear and then shuddering still. I liked his pleasure more than I'd ever thought I would. I liked that *I* made him feel that way. It was a feeling of power and pride.

When we lay there afterwards, naked, tired, and he ran his finger from my face, near my ear, down my chin, my neck, my breast, my hip, and then gave a wonderful sigh and said, "You're amazing," I knew it had been special for him, too.

# Chapter 26

I WANTED TO SPEND THE whole next day thinking about the night before, about Chris and me together. About how losing my virginity had been everything I'd wanted it to be.

But I saw Zoe and she looked awful. She walked up to me and rested her head on my shoulder.

"I feel so sick," she said, clutching her stomach. "I kept drinking after you dropped me off."

"Zoe! You need to go home." A pang of guilt hit me. I should have stayed with her instead of being with Chris.

Zoe lifted her head. "I can't. I've got two catch-rides today."

"You have to tell them you're sick. That you've got the flu."

"And never get another catch-ride again? They'll know why I can't show."

"Coffee," I said.

Zoe groaned. "Please, I've already had like three cups and

a Five-Hour Energy." She checked her phone. "I was already supposed to be on by now."

"I still think you need to throw the flag or throw in the towel, or whatever you call it."

Zoe shook her head. "Probably once I get on I'll feel better. It's kind of like a fisherman needing to be at sea. I need to be on a horse."

She didn't look particularly convincing as she said this. And the problem with the fishermen metaphor was that they weren't hung-over. I had the feeling I should do something more, but what could I do really? Zoe had gotten herself into this mess and we had already helped her out as much as we could. Maybe it was good I hadn't stayed with her last night. I was the one who told Chris she needed a wake-up call. Zoe wasn't good at taking help and so maybe she had to learn for herself to slow down. Maybe this was the wake-up call she needed and this was the time to say what I thought Chris should have said last night.

"I think you need to protect yourself a little more," I told her.

"What do you mean?"

"Last night. You were going to sleep with Trevor. You could have picked up a disease. And even if you didn't, emotionally don't you think it would have made you feel bad about yourself if you slept with him?"

"Who said I was going to sleep with him?"

I gave her a look. "Zoe, you need to think about yourself and not about guys all the time. Like maybe even take a break from guys. This is your last junior year. I know you want to win a final."

"Is that what you're doing? You didn't like Nick and you don't seem to think Teddy is good enough for you either. You think you're too good for anyone so you're going to go to college a pristine little virgin. Maybe you should consider not being so lame."

Her words hurt and I wanted to tell her about Chris and how I wasn't a virgin anymore. No, I'd lost my virginity to Chris Kern. What would she say to that?

"You're right, I'm probably a little too much the other way," I acknowledged.

"A little?" Zoe said sarcastically.

"Fine, a lot. But maybe it's better to value yourself too much than not enough."

"You are so holier-than-thou or whatever it's called," Zoe said. "I mean, get over yourself. You don't know the first thing about the circuit or any of the horse show life. I have to go ride."

Zoe turned and I called after her, "Good luck!" I wasn't trying to pick a fight with her. I just wanted to talk some sense into her.

I bought a bagel and an Odwalla smoothie at the food truck and then sat down in the front row of the stands next to the hunter ring to watch Zoe. Golf carts and the occasional dirt bike or actual bicycle were angled alongside the ring. The golf carts were filled with ring bags, grooming buckets, saddles, and even dogs. It was five minutes before the class would start. The tractor was finishing dragging the ring. Riders were warming up and Nick was calling the order of go.

"Tammy to go first. Scott in one. Then Reed in two. Helen in three. Izzy in four and Zoe in five. Let's get 'em up to the in-gate. We've got a long day ahead of us out here."

When Zoe entered the ring I had finished the bagel and was sipping my Odwalla. Jamie was at the in-gate in her usual position, arms crossed. As Zoe picked up a canter I watched to see if she was weak or not her usually focused self. But she looked okay. Maybe she'd been right about needing to be on a horse. Part of me was glad that she was fine, but there was also a part of me that wanted things to go wrong for her. How was she going to learn if she didn't suffer the consequences of her mistakes? And why did she get away with everything and the rest of us didn't?

Zoe had jumped the first fence and was cantering to the outside line. Jamie was standing with what must have been the owner of the horse she was on. Zoe rode the line well and headed down the diagonal to the in-and-out. I saw the distance coming up. It was going to be a little deep so Zoe would have to work to fit it in. Usually whenever I saw a distance that didn't look perfect somehow Zoe massaged it so it turned out amazing and it was hard to even see how she had done it because her aids were so invisible. It was sick that she was so talented, really. And that she could do it completely hung-over, no less.

Zoe neared the jump. It seemed impossible, but this time Zoe was not balancing up. Instead she legged the horse forward, trying to leave out the stride altogether. All I could think when I saw the horse lunging at the fence was that it was something I would do, not Zoe.

The horse made an effort to leave out the stride like Zoe

had asked, throwing its front feet forward, but there simply was too much ground to cover. The horse's front feet went straight into the jump. Amid rails flying, and a horse sliding, Zoe catapulted straight through the air and landed on the ground. At first no one moved except the horse who was trying to get as far away from the wreckage as possible.

I stood up, my hand to my mouth. How could I have ever wished for her to suffer the consequences of her actions? It was like I had jinxed her. What kind of friend was I?

Zoe lay on the ground as Nick called for the EMT and ran into the ring. Zoe rolled over onto her back and he told her not to move. She was clutching her shoulder. Finally, Jamie stepped into the ring. I heard her mumble, "Jesus, Zoe," as she walked toward her. A groom took the horse, which seemed thankfully unhurt, out of the ring.

The EMT arrived quickly and ran in to help Zoe. Now there was a whole group of people surrounding Zoe and I couldn't see anything for a while until someone moved and I saw Zoe's helmet was off.

I wondered whether to go into the ring, what Jamie would say, whether Zoe would want me there. She had no family here. Jamie was the closest thing to family and that was a scary thought. When I had decided I didn't care and was going to go in no matter what, Nick was calling to clear the in-gate to make way for the ambulance.

The ambulance pulled in without its lights or sirens. It looked strange to see it moving so slowly and quietly.

I got to Zoe as the EMT was telling her to lay still and explaining that they were going to move her onto a backboard.

If Zoe could hear what they were saying, she didn't acknowledge it.

"Do you want me to go with her?" I asked Jamie. I wasn't showing till later and I could miss my class anyway.

"Sure," Jamie said. She looked more annoyed than concerned.

I guess I understood why she was so mad at Zoe. It didn't take a genius to tell that she was hung-over. And Jamie did do a lot for Zoe—getting her rides, promoting her. But still, she didn't have to be so harsh. What if Zoe was really hurt? What if she'd injured her spine? I hoped the EMTs were just sticking to protocol and being overly cautious with the backboard.

I climbed in the ambulance next to Zoe. She looked so weak, strapped to the backboard, and I felt the gravitas of our friendship.

She was more lucid now; she was crying. "I know it's broken."

"What's broken?" I asked.

"My shoulder. I felt it pop when I landed. Oh my God if it's broken I won't be able to ride for weeks. What if it's not better before Regionals? It fucking kills—it's broken."

The EMT told Zoe to try to relax, and not to jump to conclusions.

"You don't know it's broken," I added. I was just glad she was talking. If it was her shoulder, she was lucky. "It might just be bruised or something."

It was a thirty-minute drive to the hospital and then I had to wait in the emergency room for another thirty minutes while the doctors saw Zoe. Word had spread across the show grounds and I got tons of texts asking if Zoe was okay, from some people I didn't even know. Both Chris and Jed asked if they should come to the hospital. I told Chris we were fine, but that I needed him to check on Logan and throw him a flake of hay. Jed wanted to come to the hospital too, but he had the Medal to show in and still needed those precious few points. I told him Zoe would be so mad if he missed the Medal to come to the hospital. The one person I didn't get a text from was Zoe's mother. I'm not sure how she would have gotten my number, but other people seemed to figure out how to get it.

When I finally got in to see her, Zoe's arm was in a sling. Her eyes were red and her cheeks streaked with tears.

"I broke my collarbone," she said, bursting into tears again.

I sat down next to her on the bed.

"How long does that take to heal?"

"Four to six weeks," Zoe said. "I shouldn't have ridden. I should have listened to you."

"You were having a really good trip," I said.

Zoe kind of laughed. "Yeah, I was. Hey, maybe I can help you some now that I'm going to be out of commission. Maybe Jamie would let me give you some lessons or something."

I felt my cheeks turn red. "Um, yeah, maybe."

I told Zoe about all the texts I had gotten, about all the people worried about her. She had me check her own phone too. There were many more texts there and I read them out loud to her. She said, "Of course just wait till the people start up saying how I can't ride and how I was drunk. And nothing from my mother, right? That figures."

I had texted Jamie to tell her Zoe was okay and to tell her I was going to skip my class and help get Zoe home. Jamie told Mike to drive over to pick us up. He drove us back to Zoe's, going extra slow so as not to jostle her. Mike didn't talk much but just the fact that he was willing to come pick us up made me think he still had feelings for Zoe.

At Zoe's condo, he asked, "Do you need me to give Logan his dinner?"

"That'd be great. Chris threw him a few flakes and checked his water, but it would be great if you could feed him and then I'll come over later and take him for a long walk and pick out his stall and stuff."

"That's so nice of Chris to do," Zoe said.

Something about the way Zoe said that made me think she thought he was doing it to help her out, which in a way he was. But it was also about me. I hung out, keeping Zoe company, watching bad reality TV, and sipping warm ginger ale. Maybe the pain meds they put her on had a little something special in them or she was wiped out because she was kind of quiet and then dozed off for a little while.

At around six, Chris showed up. I went to the door and did a bit of a double take when I saw him since he was carrying a big bouquet of flowers and take-out from the bookstore cafe. The flowers seemed like they should be for me, but I knew they weren't. I understood that giving them to Zoe was totally platonic, but still it stung a little, which I realized was stupid.

"Oh my God," Zoe said when she saw Chris. It was the most animated she had been since she'd come home. "Flowers? You are so sweet."

Her face had color again. She smoothed back her hair self-consciously. This was bad, I realized as I watched her. She thought this meant something and Chris had no idea what she was thinking. How could she think he'd be interested in her when he'd found her in a parking lot sucking off some total stranger?

Chris said, "Take-out, too. I wasn't sure what you'd feel like so I got a few different things."

Chris went into the kitchen with the take-out and flowers. I followed after him.

"How's she doing?" he asked.

"Okay." I took the flowers from him, unwrapping the cellophane. "I think she might be getting the wrong idea."

Chris turned from where he was taking out the containers of food. "About what?"

"About these." I held up the flowers. "About all of this. I think she thinks you like her."

"I do like her."

"But not as more than a friend, that's what she thinks."

Chris made a face. "No way. Zoe and I have always been friends."

"I'm just telling you what I'm seeing," I said.

Chris moved toward me and kissed me on the forehead. "Relax."

We all had dinner together and then Chris drove me back over to the horse show to take care of Logan and pick up my car. Jed was coming over to hang out with Zoe and said he'd probably sleep over just to make sure she was okay. He had gotten his last Medal points so at least something good had come out of the day.

At the show, Logan seemed happy to see me. Mike must have picked out his stall because it didn't have one piece of manure in it. I would have been worried about Logan colicking again, but I knew Mike was like that, and Logan looked perfectly fine. I told Chris I was going to take Logan out for a walk and some grass and he stayed with me. It was a beautiful night and the show grounds were empty and quiet. The sun was setting over the mountains, washing the sky with amazing pinks and purples. It was just me, Chris, and Logan, and it was perfect.

# Chapter 27

HARRIS CAME ON FRIDAY. He brought his second wife, Alexa. Looking at her, I was eternally grateful to my own father for not having gone the Twinkie route. Monica was a few years younger than my father, but not decades younger. I felt badly for Harris's children from his first marriage.

Harris was in his sixties with nearly all white hair. He was on the short side, maybe five-foot-seven, and a little thick all over. Even his face was thick and he didn't have much of a neck to speak of. His voice was funny, like he was holding his nose.

I heard him talking to Tommy Kinsler by the ring as Chris was about to get on and warm up. Alexa was with him, standing out glaringly in head-to-toe yoga clothes. She had on tight black Lululemon capri yoga pants and a tight purple tank. All she was missing was her rolled up yoga mat. On her feet she had Burberry sandals—I could tell the brand from the classic Burberry tartan pattern. I could nearly feel the sand

and grit infiltrating her toes. Every so often she'd put her foot up on the fence of the ring and bend over to touch her toe, pressing her chest to her knee. She looked so out of place and nearly everyone who came by the ring stared at her, especially when she was demonstrating her incredible flexibility. Maybe she didn't mind that—maybe getting people to stare at her was the point.

The moment Chris had his feet in the irons, Harris was excusing himself to go to the warm-up ring. Chris hadn't been kidding about Harris being so involved. Owners usually stayed in the cool and clean spectator tent, drinking bottles of chilled coconut water.

Harris watched Chris loosen up Arkos. "He feel stiff to the right?" he called out.

"Not too bad," Chris said.

I felt for Chris. He was probably dying to tell Harris to get a grip and leave him alone, but he had to indulge him and be polite while doing so.

"Looks like he's working out of it," Harris said.

I cringed for Harris. Didn't Harris know everyone in the schooling ring was inwardly laughing at him? Didn't he know he was clueless and that he would be the butt of jokes back at the tents? But would that mean Chris would be mocked too, or did they understand he *had* to put up with Harris?

Harris's phone rang and he answered just so he could loudly inform the caller that he couldn't talk because he was getting his horse ready to go into the ring. He made it sound like he was the one in the saddle.

Trevor drove by on the tractor just as Alexa was doing

some sort of backbend where she clasped her hands behind her back and essentially bent into an impossible configuration all the while throwing out her ample chest. Trevor stared, letting the tractor nearly idle. I'm sure, like every guy who saw her, he was imagining what her flexibility would be like in bed.

Chris offered to move up in the order of go and since Eve Benzinger wasn't ready, the in-gate guy let him. I think Chris took less time warming up because he wanted to get out of the schooling area. At least in the ring Harris wouldn't be able to talk to him. I hoped it wouldn't come back to haunt Chris that he'd cut his warm up short.

Arkos looked fine to the first few jumps. Harris leaned against the rail. Alexa had come to join him. I took a closer look at her sandals. They had these cute little buckles on the side. She'd probably have to throw them out after the show they'd be so trashed. She squeezed his arm as Arkos jumped, hopping up on her toes and flexing her calves, which were lean and muscled. I hated to admit it but she had an amazing body. Chris had said she was a former interior designer and Harris had met her when she was working on one of his houses. He had houses in Florida, Nantucket, and on St. Barths.

Arkos had three rails down. Again, it didn't look like Chris had made any mistakes and I couldn't tell why Arkos had rails. The only answer was that he just didn't care about clearing the jumps, but Chris had said what had drawn him to the horse in the first place was his carefulness.

Chris came out of the ring, letting the reins slip through

his fingers. He slid off and patted Arkos, which I thought was nice since I knew how disappointed Chris must be. I couldn't hear what he and Harris talked about but Harris was shaking his head. Harris and Chris got in Chris's golf cart and Alexa climbed in the back. Her posture was so good she made sitting in the back of a golf cart look like a yoga pose.

I tried not to feel left behind as they motored off to the barn. I would let them have a little time and then go see Chris.

I checked on Logan, picked two manure piles out of his stall, and gave him a flake of hay. It had been forty minutes. It had to be safe to go over now.

Chris's stalls were quiet when I got there. I didn't see anyone around, not even Dale. Jasper was in the tack room and he wagged his tail at me, which seemed like it meant he might be coming to terms with my continued presence in Chris's life, but he didn't get up. He looked hot and tired, happy to have found a piece of shade next to a tack trunk. I crouched down to pat him and that's when I heard them. Chris and Alexa.

"He listens to me. You might not think he would, but he does," Alexa was saying. "I can tell him you just need more time with Arkos."

"That's nice of you to offer," Chris said.

His voice sounded off. I stopped patting Jasper, my hand flat on his head. Chris sounded tentative, worried even, not like the Chris I knew who always sounded like he knew just what he was saying.

"I really want to help," Alexa said. "I know how difficult Harris can be."

I stood up and peered over the top of the canvas. I could see through the stall to the aisle and I could make out Alexa's purple tank. I saw her glossy black hair and then Chris's hand on her shoulder, pushing her away.

"Alexa," he said. "I'm flattered but—"

"Let me help you," she said. "Let me make you feel good."

Before I could think more about it, I tore around the aisle. Jasper came with me. "Chris, Jamie needs to see you. She sent me over. It's . . . it's something about the NARG. The emergency meeting?"

During my online fact-finding about Chris, I had read he was a member of the North American Riders Group. Of course, there was no emergency meeting and Jamie wasn't involved. But it sounded good. Alexa wouldn't know any better. And I had to get Chris out of there.

"Okay, thanks," Chris said. To Alexa, he said, "I gotta go. I'll see you later."

When we were far enough away in Chris's golf cart, Jasper riding on the back, he said, "Thank you. You saved me."

"Was she doing what I think she was doing?"

"Throwing herself at me? Yes, and it's not the first time."

"You're not, um, interested, are you?" I thought of Alexa's body, of her legs and her perfectly sculpted butt in her yoga pants. It wasn't just Trevor who had been staring—there were plenty of guys at the show who would have loved to have Alexa coming on to them.

"No, are you kidding me? But I can't offend her or tell

Harris. This is such a disaster. I'm going to have to tell Dale he can't leave me alone for a second all weekend."

"Harris really thinks he's a trainer, too, huh?"

Chris shook his head. "Maybe I could get him off my back if the horse would leave the rails up."

I put my hand on his shoulder. "You'll figure him out. I know you will."

"Thanks," Chris said.

# Chapter 28

WHEN I JUMPED THE LAST FENCE, I let out a gasp. It was like I had been holding my breath for the whole course and could finally breathe. I loosened my reins and let Logan walk out of the ring on a long stride. He lowered his head, shook it gently once, and walked on.

"Not bad," Jamie said. "Not bad."

Not bad? Up until the last few weeks it had seemed utterly impossible that Logan would ever go well in the ring, or that I would ever come off course feeling exhilarated, not upset. I had put in a bunch of respectable four-fault rounds and this was my first ever entirely clear round, which meant I'd made it into the jump-off for the first time ever. I'd been so surprised and nervous, I'd worried I wouldn't remember the shortened course. But somehow I'd managed to get the jumps in the right order and not knock any down. My time was slow but I had been clear.

"I must say, Hannah, I'm pleasantly surprised. These weeks of practice have obviously done you well."

Zoe was standing next to Jamie. Lately that's where Zoe always was.

"Great," Zoe said, looking at Jamie and then at me. "Big improvement."

At first it had been strange to see Zoe at the horse show and not in boots and breeches. But now I was used to seeing her in civilian clothes, which today meant a pair of khaki shorts and a pink tank top. Her arm that wasn't in the sling was still red and scabby from the accident on the alpine slides.

"We've still got some work to do," Jamie said. "But we've come this far. It's a good start."

I smiled at Jamie, but I really felt like laughing. I wanted to tell her all about Chris, about the secret lessons, so Jamie would know the truth; that it was Chris who was teaching me how to ride.

When Jamie got into her golf cart, Zoe said, "God, Hannah, that was really good. I mean, seriously."

"Thanks." I wanted to look around to see if Chris had been watching. But I didn't want to make it obvious that I was looking for him.

"I'm actually kind of amazed. I mean, I hope that doesn't sound bad. It's just such a major improvement."

"Thanks," I said again. "For once I felt—"

The in-gate guy's voice cut me off. "We have only four more left here to go in the children's jumper class. Four more to go before we reset the course for the Junior/Amateur-Owner lows and walk it."

"I better head back to hunter land," Zoe said. "We've got one going in the ponies. Jamie probably needs my help."

"I guess I'll stick around . . . see if I get a ribbon, which would be a total miracle."

Zoe did a little excited dance, pumping her fists.

"Hey," I called as she walked away. "Have you seen Chris?"

The moment the words were out of my mouth I was kicking myself. Why couldn't I have just kept quiet? Zoe stopped and put her hand on her hip. "No, why?"

I shrugged. "Just wondering. That's all."

I looked back at the course I'd just ridden and felt a zap of excitement that I'd ridden it so well. I played back my mental video, reliving each jump. It was something I didn't usually do. Usually I tried desperately to rid my mind of the images.

When I had come out of the ring, the announcer had said that I was standing in fifth place. Since then a few other horses had gone clean and made it into the jump-off. I had lost track of their times while I talked to Jamie but now with only a few left to go, I couldn't help but wonder if I would get a ribbon.

When the last horse finished the course, the announcer said, "That was our last to go here in class number 18, the children's jumper class. Results coming right up."

When the results were announced, I listened to each name, my fingers clenched on the reins. As the fourth place was awarded, my stomach fluttered.

"In fifth place we have . . . number 390, Katherine Gibson . . ."

My stomach dropped. Come on, just one little ribbon.

"And in sixth place is number 572, Hannah Waer aboard

Personal Best. Personal Best is owned by Stephen Waer from Palo Alto, California."

As I walked Logan up to the in-gate to get my ribbon from Tucker, the jumper in-gate guy, my whole body felt like it was glowing. I had done it; I had finally gotten a ribbon. But the main person I had to thank and the one person I wanted to see was nowhere in sight.

* * *

Chris was sitting on my tack trunk when I came back to the barn. "I was wondering when you were going to decide to come back."

I held up the green ribbon and smiled. "Look!"

"I know. I heard it announced. Your first ribbon."

"Well, not ever. I'm not that big a dork."

"I know that."

I led Logan into the grooming stall and started to un-tack him. Chris stood up to help me.

"So, how'd it feel out there?"

"Good. Much more solid."

Chris nodded. "It looked it."

"But . . . ? C'mon, I know there's always a but."

"But we still need to work on regulating his stride. Did you feel how sometimes you had everything in control like through the five line and all the way to the single oxer?"

"Uhuh."

"That's how he needs to feel all the time. You lost him a little to the double, right? He got a little fast on you. A little anxious and he started to pull."

"I tried to sit up and half-halt."

"I know, I saw. But that's where we need to put in more hours on the flat because he doesn't always respond right away. He still needs to learn what you're asking him to do."

"Right," I said.

"And it was your first jump-off—"

I cut him off. "So I'm just glad I remembered where I was going!"

"I know. I was kind of worried about that."

"But I was too slow, right?"

"You were fine for your first jump-off. Plus, it's not all about speed; it's about the track between the jumps. But all in all, it was a super ride."

I leaned against Logan's shoulder and sighed. "Wait till my dad hears this."

Chris put his hand to Logan's chest.

"Is he still hot?" I asked.

"He's pretty cool. Let's put him in his stall for a few minutes so we can gloat?"

"Good idea." I led Logan into his stall and then sat down on the trunk with Chris.

"You were awesome," he said.

"Really?"

Chris put his hand on my waist. "Really."

"It's all thanks to you . . . Without your help every morning, without your lessons—"

I closed my eyes, already feeling woozy, ready to kiss Chris. What could be better? Riding a good round, getting a ribbon that my dad would be proud of, and getting to come back to the barn and kiss my gorgeous grand prix rider boyfriend? Instead I felt Chris's hand tighten on my waist. I opened my eyes to see Zoe standing in the entrance to the tent.

"Congratulations, you guys," she said. "I guess it was a group effort."

I smiled and Chris did his cute thing where he threw back his head and laughed. He said, "Well, I guess now you know."

Her voice was fake chipper. "Yeah, now I know. So you've been helping her. That's why she's gotten so much better."

"You won't—" I said.

"Tell?" Zoe said. "No, you guys are safe. I won't tell."

"Hey," Chris said. "How about celebrating tonight? You, me, Jed, and Hannah?"

"Yeah," I said.

Zoe shook her head. "I can't. I'm supposed to stay late, help Jamie."

"We could go late," I said.

"Nah, that's okay. Some other time."

Zoe gave us one last look that said it wasn't fine, not fine at all. "See you."

"I think I better just make sure this is okay," I told Chris as I stood up to go after Zoe.

"I'm sure it's all good. Don't worry."

"I'm just going to make sure." For someone who was really smart and good with horses, Chris didn't seem to have much intuition when it came to people and the dynamics between them. This was so not fine. I caught up to Zoe outside the tent. "Is everything okay?"

"Sure. Why wouldn't it be?"

"I don't know. You seem kind of, kind of—"

Zoe shook her head, her ponytail bouncing. "I have to go help Jamie. You know since I can't ride, since I fucked that up, I figure I have to do whatever else I can."

Zoe started walking again and I kept up with her.

"So, Chris has been helping you, huh?" she said.

"Yeah."

"What, like every morning or something?"

"Pretty much."

"Since when?"

"Since the day after you introduced me to him at the bar." I realized as I said it that I'd been lying by omission to Zoe for a long time now.

"Cool," Zoe said. "That's . . . wow. Cool. And when did it become something more?"

I felt myself blushing. "I don't know. Maybe two weeks now. It just sort of happened. I never would have thought . . ."

"Are you having sex with him?" Zoe stopped and looked at me, her eyes accusatory. "You did. You lost your virginity to him." Somehow just by looking at me, she could tell.

"Yes," I admitted. "I'm so sorry I didn't tell you . . . don't you think he was a good choice?"

She shrugged. "Sure, why not. I mean, it'll be over when Circuit ends anyway. There's no way Chris would be serious about you, but that's what you planned all along."

"Yeah," I said, my heart sinking. "Right."

Zoe motioned to the schooling ring where Jamie was getting a rider ready. "I really better go."

I watched Zoe walk away, her stride purposeful. Why did it *have* to be over when Circuit ended? It had only just begun. Zoe's words had brought up everything I had tried not to think about. Was this just a summer thing with Chris? Was that what he thought it was? And even if it could be something more, how would that ever work with him on the show circuit and me in college?

# Chapter 29

THE SUMMER SO FAR had been full of surprises. One of the biggest surprises was that I came to take unexpected pleasure in barn work. The details mattered to me. I found I actually liked cleaning my tack, and I was obsessive about getting it squeaky clean, the leather glowing and supple, and the bit and stirrup irons gleaming. I loved crossing the throatlatch and securing the noseband so the bridle looked impeccably neat when hung up.

I became just as enamored with cleaning Logan's stall. I loved the way it looked with the fresh shavings perfectly banked. Anytime he'd manure, I'd be in there quickly picking it out. Besides organizing the feed, supplements, and grooming box, my other obsession became raking the aisle. There was nothing better than when it was just raked. The grass that had been there when we'd first arrived had long disappeared, leaving a layer of sandy dirt. I learned from watching Mike that I should spray the aisle with a little water first and then rake. I always raked right to left, creating artistic fan designs worthy of any Japanese rock garden.

I learned to take care of Logan with the same attention to detail. I dedicated myself to having him clean and I was proud of how perfect he looked when we went out for a hack. I'd learned from Mike about supplements and grain and I learned from watching the farrier about hoof care. I had learned about all sorts of tack now and was even adept at putting much of it on. I never flatted Logan now without a belly band or ear bonnet. I felt like everywhere I went at the show I could pick up tidbits about horse care if I just paid attention and was willing to ask questions. I could never have predicted I'd care about any of the parts of horse care. I thought I'd do the bare minimum to survive, but I relished doing it all to perfection and I took great satisfaction in the fact that I had become a fanatical and fantastic groom. Smells non-horse people would have hated, I now loved. Fly spray and Show Sheen and Logan when he was sweaty. Even manure didn't smell bad to me, if I was being completely honest. I could have worn fly spray as perfume I loved the smell so much.

For the first time, I could really understand why people like Mike or Dale enjoyed their job so much. I used to wonder how anyone could enjoy taking care of a horse and never once riding it or showing it, but now it made perfect sense. I actually thought if I had to choose—riding or grooming—I'd choose grooming.

At the end of the day on Sunday, Chris rode by my aisle on Arkos. "Wanna go for a hack?" he asked.

"Sure," I said. "I just have to tack up."

"I'll wait," Chris said.

Logan was already clean so all I had to do was throw on

his bridle and saddle. I mounted up and Chris and I headed off side-by-side.

"Where are we going?" I asked.

"Just around the grounds," he said. "I know where I'm going."

We passed the back tents and the guy who sold tacos and burritos out of his truck that the grooms loved. Music spilled out of the last tent, MISSION by Low Flying Planes. Ever since we'd gone to the rodeo, I kept hearing that song again and again. It had became the unofficial song of the summer— played on both the country and pop stations. Just that morning, I'd heard it on the way to the show. Then I'd heard it coming out of the food truck when I went to get lunch, and Mike had been singing it as he led Hobbes up to the ring for Zoe for the junior hunters. I knew every word now—it was a highly sing-able song. When I heard it in the car, I would turn it up and sing along loudly. It was definitely overplayed and maybe some people even came to hate it that summer, but not me. I couldn't get enough of it. I knew that the song would be forever linked with those weeks in Vermont, and with my time with Chris. I'd hear it when I was at Tufts in the middle of the winter, and I'd be right back in the mountains of Vermont, with the open sky and the constant sound of the horse show announcer, and Chris. The smell of Chris, what it felt like to lie next to him, what it felt like to know he was my boyfriend. Of course I thought, or hoped, that he would be my boyfriend in the coming months, and maybe we'd be together for the rest of my life. But no matter what would happen, or how old I was—twenty, thirty, forty even—that song would always take me back to those weeks and him.

We walked as far as we could, past the back ring with the sign that read LUNGEING ONLY. The tents became blocks of blue and white in the distance. It was nice to get away from the show and all the people and horses crowded into such a small space. When the show had first started, all the grass around the rings and in front of the tents had been green and lush. Now most were burnt out brown, if there was any grass left at all. It had become harder and harder to find a place to graze.

A small river ran along the back of the show grounds and we followed it for a time. The water was low since it had been a dry month and big rocks poked out of the riverbed. We came to a point in the river where the riverbed was low and there weren't many rocks and Chris suggested we take the horses in the river. I had never ridden a horse in water before and I certainly didn't know if Logan would even go.

Chris led. Arkos plunked into the water happily, stretching out his nose. Logan seemed surprised, stretching up in his neck. But he followed willingly. We stopped in the middle of the river, the water up to the horses' knees.

"He likes it," I said, as Logan too sniffed the water. His breath disturbed the surface and he pulled back, surprised. Then he tried it again, this time dipping his lip and then his nose into the water. He moved his lips around, nudging the water. He flipped his head, spraying water back at Chris and me. "I guess he really likes it."

Arkos started pawing, splashing the water about. It was

so cute to see the horses playing, having fun and being regular horses, not just show horses.

"Do you ever get nervous?" I asked Chris. "I mean for the grand prix?"

"Of course. But it's part of the whole thing—you have to learn how to deal with the nerves and in a way they can help you ride better."

Chris told me about what he'd heard of how the U.S. Team had fared at Dublin that weekend. Mary Beth wasn't on that squad—she had gone on the developing team that competed at smaller venues in Europe. I tried to imagine Chris in Europe, competing in famous shows like Aachen and Rotterdam against all the biggest names in show jumping.

"So what's your dream? To win the World Cup, or go to the Olympics?"

"Yeah, I definitely want that. I also want my own farm and I want to own my own horses, but that's probably not very realistic when a grand prix horse costs ten million dollars."

"Ten million?" I had heard people talking at the in-gate one day about Adele Bonderman's horse that had sold for eight million to the Saudi team, but I'd thought that was just gossip.

"Well, for an Olympic horse, yeah."

"What about Mary Beth? Who buys her horses?"

"Her parents are independently wealthy."

"That helps."

"Yeah, it helps a lot."

Logan poked his nose in the water again. I wanted to ask

Chris what would happen after Circuit, but I didn't want to ruin the moment. Or maybe I didn't want to hear the inevitable truth—that like the song on the radio, things between us wouldn't last.

# Chapter 30

OF COURSE MY DAD couldn't tell me in advance he was coming to visit. He had to text me from the airport in Burlington, VT.

HAD A BREAK IN MY SCHEDULE. JUST LANDED IN BURLINGTON. BE TO THE SHOW IN AN HOUR.

What? He would be here in an hour?

I was showing later and I had felt fine about it. Things had been going so well for Logan and me. Last Sunday, I had only four faults in the children's and I'd gone double clear in the 1.00 meter class. I'd texted my dad and I'd been so proud of how I was doing. I was not only surviving the horse show on my own, I was killing it.

But now I was a bundle of nerves. My dad would be here to watch. He would stand at the ring, his eyes glued to me. Seeing was believing. He wanted to see for himself that I was really succeeding. Now I just had to show him.

I was waiting for my turn to go. I scanned the sides of the ring. Chris had started watching me that very first day, the day I didn't even get around the course, and since the secret lessons he had always been at the ring when I rode. I checked his usual spots, by the spectator tent and in the stands, but he wasn't in either place and he also hadn't responded to my texts. I looked down at Logan's neck and laced my fingers through his mane. So the day my dad comes, Chris decides to disappear. Was it because he didn't want to meet my dad? He hadn't said anything about it. We'd spent all of Monday and Tuesday together, hanging out, having sex sometimes two times a day, and watching episodes of HOUSE OF CARDS when Chris wasn't looking at horses online. Things had seemingly been so perfect between us.

Dad was standing a few feet from the in-gate. He didn't do casual clothes well and today's outfit was no exception—a dark colored running shirt made out of some tech-fabric paired with long boarder shorts that I could imagine a store clerk telling him looked good on him. Why didn't Monica help him buy his clothes? Because she was too busy working till all hours, which was also why she hadn't accompanied him on this trip. Despite his clothes, my dad was good-looking. He was thin and fit and he had that air of confidence of men who've made their own fortune. Perhaps men who have family money have an air about them too, but my dad had a certain way of looking at the world—an I-made-it-without-you attitude. Right now he also looked impatient. The whole horse show thing didn't make sense to him. A race where dozens of horses started off at the same time and you could tell who was winning made sense. But a whole ring full of jumps saved for one rider at a time defied his sense of practicality and expediency. All the waiting around at horse shows went against his very DNA of Getting Things Done As Quickly and Efficiently as Possible.

"Hannah's on deck," Philip said.

I tried to think of the course, but the only thoughts that raced through my mind were unrelated to the jumps ahead. Why wasn't Chris watching? Why hadn't I seen him since my lesson that morning? Why hadn't he returned any of my texts? Had I done something wrong?

"You know where you're going out there?" Jamie asked as the in-gate guy, Philip said, "Hannah, you're in."

Ever since I'd started hanging out with Zoe and Jed and Chris I'd become one of the in-crowd at the horse show. One of the people Philip knew by name. It felt good to be one of the insiders, but fragile in a way too. Would Philip remember me after the summer? How many people were in the in-crowd for a summer or a year, and then just dropped out of the horse show world altogether?

"Show me what you can do out there," Dad said. "I'm watching."

As if there was any confusion over that last part.

I waited for the tone and then picked up a trot. I headed down the long side of the ring, surprised at how stiff I felt. It was like my arms were frozen and my knees bolted to the saddle.

It was only twenty seconds before I was at the first jump but in that short time so many thoughts went through my head. First, I tried to pretend he wasn't watching, that he hadn't just said what he had said, but it was impossible. Then

I started thinking about Chris, and where the hell was he when I needed him? Zoe wasn't here to support me either but she had been acting funny ever since she'd seen Chris and me kissing. She'd been acting like she was too busy to do anything but be Jamie's right hand girl.

I thought of my mom and her birds. No wonder my dad had picked up and left. Who wanted to be married to the bird-woman? It was so unfair that he could come watch me when her anxiety kept her a prisoner at home.

I didn't pick up the canter until I was almost around the corner to the first jump. I was sure I could hear Jamie and maybe my dad too saying, "What the hell is she waiting for?" I didn't really know what I was waiting for. Maybe for things to settle down in my head or maybe for Chris to show up. The only good thing about having picked up the canter so late was that there wasn't much time before the first jump. I was there before I knew what had happened and somehow I was all right when I landed on the other side even though I had absolutely no recollection of how I had made it over.

The second jump was fine too. I glided to it, not even knowing that I had turned the corner and steered to the line. My arms still felt frozen and my legs weak, but somehow I was on and still riding. I made it almost all the way around the course like that—feeling like things were going slowly and quickly at the same time. The second to last jump was a long approach to a triple bar, with three separate rails on three sets of standards, each a few inches higher than the other. At first I saw the triple bar as it was, like the slant of a ladder, but then the rails started to blur together. I glanced away from the jump for a split second and then back to it again, but it still looked fuzzy. I wondered if I had time to look at my dad at the side of the ring or to check for Chris again and then I realized that the blur was getting closer. I would have to jump it, even if I couldn't quite see it. There were only a few more strides left to go.

At the last stride, Logan veered to the right, flinging me to the left and onto the ground, just missing the rails of the jump. I landed with a thud that somehow seemed to snap me out of my dream-like paralysis. At first I felt almost relieved— I had ridden exactly like my father expected I would. Terribly. But then I felt a wave of anger pass through me. I held my hand up to my mouth and closed my eyes. I had failed. I had failed myself again. I could have done it—I knew I could have conquered that course just like I had the past few times in the ring. But instead I had let it get to me, let him get to me, let myself get to me, and I had fallen apart.

I rose slowly. Logan was cantering around the ring with his reins drooping dangerously low on one side and Jamie was walking toward me. If my dad weren't there, she wouldn't have bothered.

"You all right?" she said.

I nodded. I was fine actually, which was nearly annoying. Suddenly I wished I was in horrible pain or had broken something semi-serious. If I couldn't impress him I could at least spark his sympathy. Logan came to a stop on the far side of the ring. He let Jamie approach him, take the reins over his head, and walk him out of the ring. When we were outside and away from the in-gate, Jamie handed me the reins.

"What were you thinking?"

"I don't know."

I felt a hand on my shoulder. "What were you doing out there, kiddo?" My father glanced to Jamie. "Am I wrong, or wasn't the distance right there?"

I stiffened under his touch. This from the man who had only sat on a horse once in his life at a dude ranch he took me and Ryan to out west. And I distinctly remember his horse kept lunging for grass and pulling the reins out of his hands, which drove him crazy. He hated that there were no buttons to press, no code to learn. Yet he had seen the distance I should have seen.

"You looked like you were just sitting up there waiting for it all to work out for you," Jamie said. "You have to ride each jump."

"Did she really get a ribbon last week?" my dad asked her.

"I should get him back to the barn," I said, motioning to Logan. "I don't have a groom anymore, you know."

"Right. I'll be there in a few minutes."

I led Logan toward the barn. He sighed once like he understood what a disappointment the whole thing was. Like he knew we should have done better. I patted his neck—it was my fault, not his. Logan and I had become a pair. We were on the same side now. He had even reduced his water bucket pooping to only once a week, at most.

Back at the barn, still no Chris. Still no Zoe. She was clearly avoiding me since Jamie had been helping me, but Zoe wasn't there when Zoe was always by her side these days. I stripped the tack off Logan and went about putting him away. It was nice to lose myself in the physical part of taking care of him. I had hated that part so much in the beginning, but now there was comfort in brushing him and doing up his legs, especially when it kept my mind from thinking about what my dad was talking to Jamie about at the ring.

My dad still hadn't reappeared by the time I had Logan all brushed down and his legs wrapped. The tears I was trying to hold back started running down my cheeks. I put Logan in his stall and sat down on my trunk. I took a towel and wiped my face. The only thing worse than crying was crying when you felt embarrassed to be crying in the first place. I was being such a baby. It was like my dad brought out the worst in me. I wanted to show him what I had become here in Vermont, but suddenly I was the old-me again.

Before I even knew where I was going, I was jogging out of the tent over to Chris's stalls.

Chris was sitting in one of the director's chairs, with his feet on the coffee table and his head tilted back. A very un-Chris pose. He looked defeated, overwhelmed. Eduardo, one of his grooms, Dale, and Jasper were with him. As I came closer, Dale elbowed Chris. Chris sat up and put his hands on his knees.

I stopped in front of him. "I was looking for you. Where were you? Did you see my round? Did you watch?"

Chris looked at Dale, like he was waiting for some kind of signal of what to say or how to act, and then back at me. "I had to ride."

"But you said you—"

Chris stood up. "Actually we've got to go find Doc Sheridan. Maybe I'll see you later."

I started backing away from the tent. It was amazing how much could be said with so few words. He might as well have said: I made a mistake with you. A big one. And now I don't want to have anything more to do with you. This was the same man I'd had sex with not even twenty-four hours ago.

"Sure. Maybe later," I said, although it was clear this was not a to-be-continued. But there was so much he wasn't saying. Why? What happened?

I walked back to my stalls slowly. My head was throbbing. I looked at the ground as I walked, watching my feet step, one and then the other.

# Chapter 31

MY DAD GLANCED BACK AND FORTH between his phone and the road as we drove to the restaurant, holding the steering wheel with a knee and a wrist, his phone perched on the top of the wheel.

"I thought teenagers were the ones who were supposed to have a problem with texting and driving."

"I can't get any service at my hotel. All my emails just came in—hundreds of them."

God forbid he didn't answer them right away. And he had to point out how there were *hundreds* of them—like it was some popularity contest. Sometimes my dad seemed worse than a teenager.

The road became winding and he had to concentrate on driving. He put his phone in the front console but he kept looking longingly at it every so often, like it had him brainwashed and was calling out to him in a language only audible to him and whales.

The restaurant was fancy. My dad pretended to not be a

foodie—who had time to care about eating when you had a business to run? But come on, he lived in Palo Alto, even mediocre places there had good food. The few times I'd visited we'd eaten a lot of organic, farm-to-table, saffron-infused food. I liked that kind of food too, but I didn't like how my dad pretended he'd be fine with any old burger and then just wasn't.

He ordered the tuna and had to discuss it with the waiter first, making sure it would be seared. Then out of nowhere when I was listening to him tell me all about Ryan and his latest venture, my dad called the waiter back over and canceled the order, choosing the brick-grilled organic young chicken instead. The waiter stuttered, trying to figure out whether he could send back a probably already prepped meal and my dad explained he'd pay for both, just don't bring the tuna. It was the right thing to do, I guess, but it was annoying too. *I have so much money that I can change my mind and order two meals if I want. Let some lucky schmuck dishwasher eat my discarded tuna.*

When the waiter left, Dad said to me, "I don't know what I was thinking ordering seafood so far from the ocean. I've been going so hard lately. I think I forgot where I was for a moment."

I began to say I was sure they shipped it up here and it was still fresh, but then I realized, why bother? He was such a snob, making the point of how California was so much better than poor landlocked Vermont.

Over salads, I heard more about Ryan. He was preparing to go out for a round of funding. My dad was helping him where he could, but he wasn't putting him in touch with anyone. "He has to do that on his own."

Somehow with the last name Waer I had the feeling VCs would take my brother's call. And Ryan wasn't dumb—he'd use Dad's name if he had to.

Dad checked his phone. I rearranged my silverware. I could have checked my own phone, but I didn't want to stoop to his level and plus, I didn't need to be reminded that Chris hadn't texted me.

He finally put his down. "Jamie says you're improving, not considering today, of course."

"Definitely. Today was just like a blip or something."

"An aberration."

I nodded and wondered why it was that when I was with my father my words always got tangled.

"And Jamie? It's working out with her? No more from this, this other rider or whoever it was your mom was carping about?"

I looked away. Chris should have been here with me, having dinner with my father. Instead, I was facing him alone. "Nope, no more of that."

"We need to talk about what to do with Logan in the fall," Dad said.

"I guess I thought you'd still keep him with Jamie. Campus isn't that far away from the barn."

"I'm thinking of the value proposition. That doesn't make sense."

Why did my dad always have to talk in business terms? My mom talked incessantly about birds and my dad used business lingo. Couldn't someone talk like a normal person? Logan was a horse; not a value proposition.

"Now you want to sell him?"

"If he's going well, or at least better, it would seem prudent."

I looked up at the ceiling and shook my head. "You get me this horse I hate and who hates me. I can't ride him to save my life. You send me off to a show and make me take care of him by myself for weeks when I've never even taken care of a hamster. Then, you know what? I actually get good at taking care of him. I begin to get good at riding him. And I like him. For the first time since Dobby I actually *like* my horse. Maybe I even love him. And now—" I made a dramatic show of pretending to rip a rug out from under someone. "Now it's, let's sell him."

It hit me hard right then how much I did love Logan. I couldn't have him taken away from me. And not now, not when I was possibly losing Chris. There were only two more weeks of the circuit—what would I have left?

"Okay, so pitch me." He leaned back in his chair, all SHARK TANK. "What do we do with him? You'll be immersed in school. It costs thousands of dollars a month to keep him at Jamie's. What's your plan?"

"How can I have a plan? I just found out you want to sell him."

"You have to be thinking ahead—always running through the possible scenarios and planning your response to what you think someone might do."

The waiter arrived with our entrees. He seemed to have a

proud look on his face, like he had rolled with the punches, and was now delivering just what my dad wanted. What he didn't know was that the rules changed all the time with my dad. What worked one minute would be scrapped the next. The waiter slid the plate in front of my dad. He studied it, like he was assessing more than food.

"This looks great," I said about my meal to distract the waiter away from my dad. "Thank you."

The waiter gave me a grateful smile and eased away, probably realizing that he should escape before my dad pulled something else.

"Okay, you have time," Dad said. "Figure out a plan. But remember, thinking on the fly is key." He tapped his own head.

"Key to what?" I asked.

"Life. It's the key to life."

# Chapter 32

MY NEXT FEW DAYS AT THE SHOW were painfully quiet. No more early morning lessons. I had shown up several times at our usual time and spot—no Chris. No texts from Chris. No texts from Zoe. When I saw Zoe, she was cordial but nothing more. Everything had changed between us. Chris and I didn't usually cross paths much unless I tried to be where he was, which I had spent the past few weeks getting very good at. Now, though, I stayed away from the grand prix ring and the grand prix schooling area. I went to the general store for lunch so I wouldn't run into him at the food truck.

Saturday came and went and I heard the announcer calling out about the course walk for the grand prix. Only once the class had started did I walk to the ring and sit in the back row of the stands, where Chris wouldn't see me. He didn't ride well. In fact, he rode the worst I'd ever seen him ride. That didn't mean he made a big mistake—had a major chip or a refusal. But something in the way he rode didn't look right. He was off and he had three rails with Titan. As he left the ring, his shoulders were hunched and he kept his eyes down. Of course I couldn't help but wonder if his performance had to do with missing me. But that was probably ascribing too much weight to our relationship.

I made sure Chris had left the grand prix area before I headed back to the barn. As I got down from the stands I saw two juniors pointing at me. One whispered something to the other. Why the hell were they pointing at me and what were they whispering about? Was our break-up the talk of the show now? How could it have been since as far as I knew hardly anyone knew about us in the first place? Still, I quickly turned away from them, feeling self-conscious and awful, like I'd done something wrong. I imagined their voices: *That's her. Chris was sleeping with her? What the hell was he thinking?*

I saw Jed ahead of me and I jogged to catch up with him. It wasn't often that I found him without Zoe and I was grabbing my chance—Jed knew *everything*.

"Hey," I said.

"Oh, hi," Jed said.

"Did you watch the grand prix?"

Jed nodded, but didn't speak. Was talking to me making him uncomfortable? Why was everyone acting so weird all of a sudden?

"Chris didn't ride very well."

"Yeah, wasn't his day," Jed said.

He was being cool, stand-off-ish. No easy smiles, no automatic jokes. Jed was acting like someone close to him had died.

"Can I ask you something?" I said. Before he could say no

or tell me he was late to be somewhere I continued, "Does Zoe hate me now?"

"It's complicated." We had reached the general vicinity of the tents and Jed stopped, like he didn't want to go any further toward the barn until he had gotten rid of me.

"What the hell is going on?" I said. "It's like the whole *horse show* hates me now. What did I do?"

Jed gazed at me, like he was trying to figure out how to put something into words, or maybe just trying to figure out if I could be trusted, or whether he wanted to help me.

"Please," I said. "I'm like freaking out here because I have no idea what's going on. Chris has stopped talking to me. Zoe barely says a word to me. People are pointing at me . . ."

"It's not a good world, Hannah," he said.

"What do you mean?"

"The horse show world. It'll eat you up and spit you out."

I was already figuring that one out. But I, at least, wanted to know why. What had I done that made them want to eat me up and spit me out? Was it because Chris was one of their own and I was just some for-the-summer interloper? Was it because of Mary Beth and something about her coming back and wanting Chris back? I was grasping for reasons where none seemed to exist.

"I gotta go," Jed said.

"No, Jed, come on," I pleaded. "Just tell me the truth. I can handle it, I swear."

"Zoe and I go back forever," he said. "I'm sorry." And he walked away from me.

I wanted to yell after him, to tell him to wait, to tell him he couldn't do this to me. That I needed one person to be honest with me and he seemed like he should be that person. What did he mean by saying he and Zoe went back forever? Zoe was mad at me for sleeping with Chris when she liked him, and then not telling her, and Jed could only pick one side—hers or mine? All I knew was something serious was going on—I had apparently done something horrible.

* * *

It was awful sitting at home, knowing Sunday night was happening at Backcountry. I went to check on Logan, intensely glad to have something to do. I turned off my high beams upon entering the show grounds and drove slowly over to the tent. Since no one else was there, I parked close to the tent and turned off the engine.

The weak overhead lamps in the tents that stayed on all night made it light enough for me to find my way to Logan's stall. As I approached, I couldn't see Logan. I looked over the stall door and found him curled up on the ground like a deer.

"Psst," I whispered. "Logan?"

He lifted up his head. He had been asleep—he wasn't sick. There were shavings stuck on his chin from where it had rested on the floor of the stall. Adorable. Once he saw me, his wide eyes softened.

"I'm sorry I woke you." At least one of us looked relaxed and happy. I spoke softly to him as I opened the door and walked toward him. "Don't get up. Don't worry."

I walked slowly into the stall, crouching down with each

step. I kneeled by his neck, running my fingers through his mane. At first I could tell Logan wasn't quite sure what to think, what was going on, but as I rubbed his neck, his body relaxed and he lowered his chin back onto the stall floor. Every few seconds his eyes blinked shut at the same time that one of his ears twitched. I ran my hand all the way up to Logan's ears since his head was low enough to touch them. Logan's ears flicked forward. Had my dad bought Logan for me to watch me fail? It was an awful thought. And now that I was succeeding, did he want to sell him out from under me? Even if it wasn't true, the fact that I would wonder said a lot about our relationship.

Logan rested his face against my stomach and his nostrils fluttered against my shirt. If Logan was a test, I had passed.

I pressed my face to Logan's neck. "I don't hate you at all." I felt like I had lost so much, but I still had Logan.

I took the long way by Backcountry and saw all the cars in the lot. I was tempted to stop and look for Chris's car or Zoe's or Jed's, but that felt stalker-ish, too insane even for me given the circumstances.

So instead I went back to the condo. Cheryl was out, of course. Everyone was out. It was only me sitting on my bed, wondering why the world hated me.

I tried to go to bed, but I couldn't sleep. I turned over and back and over again, the sheets now tangled up by my feet. I rolled onto my back and threw off the covers so they landed on the floor. Had I even been asleep at all? I checked the clock. 1:37. I sat up, ran my hands through my hair, then lunged out of bed. *Life*, my dad had said, *thinking on your feet was the key to life*. Maybe the key to life was also being brave.

I threw on a pair of jeans, a long sleeve T-shirt and a hoodie. In the bathroom, I pulled my hair back into a ponytail that fell all the way past my shoulders even though it was set up high on my head. As I looked at myself in the mirror, I paused. I stared at myself, at my green eyes and pale skin that was now dotted with freckles from the summer. I wondered whether it could ever have been true, that Chris once liked me? That I had once wondered whether we could have been falling in love.

I drove over to Chris's and I knocked hard against the door. I took a step back, listened, then knocked again, this time louder. I heard movement inside and then saw a light click on in the hallway leading to the bedroom, where we had had sex so many times, and then one went on in the front hall.

Chris opened the door. He had on a T-shirt and striped boxers and his hair was mashed to one side. He wiped his hand across his face and shook his head.

"What are you doing here?" he said.

"I don't get what happened between us."

Chris let out an exaggerated breath. "Really, Hannah? I thought you were better than most show people."

"I am, I mean I think I am."

"Then why tell the whole world about it? I thought we had something special."

"I did too. And I didn't tell the whole world. I didn't tell anybody. Zoe asked me after she saw us kissing and I told her how long we had been, well, you know, and that we'd, that I'd had sex with you."

Why were the words coming out so awful? I sounded so stupid, so young.

"A SUMMER OF HORSE SHOW FIRSTS?" Chris said.

"I have no idea what you're talking about," I replied.

"You wrote about all of it, everything between us."

I still didn't know what he was referring to, but the fuzzy outlines were taking shape like a dot-to-dot when you're halfway done and you begin to see the picture of what you're drawing. "Zoe," I said. Somehow I knew she was responsible for whatever Chris was talking about.

Chris must have believed in that moment that maybe I hadn't done whatever terrible thing was out there because his face softened. The old Chris I knew, the kind, open face I'd looked at when we had slept together, returned just a little bit. I took my opening. "Can you show me whatever it is you're talking about?"

Chris opened the door all the way to let me in. It felt like a big step forward. We went to his laptop. A couple clicks and the screen was open.

A SUMMER OF HORSE SHOW FIRSTS

*My name is Hannah and I'm 18, but before this summer I had never had sex. I was a virgin. But then I met Chris Kern. I fell hard for Chris and I decided this was the summer every-thing would change for me. I made it my sole purpose to get him to fall for me. To get him to sleep with me. To get him to take away my virginity. He was way out of my league but I had to have him. Chris was up for it in every sense of the word too. I think he likes younger girls because it turned out to be easier than I thought it would be . . .*

My hand flew to my mouth as I read. At the same time, I felt sick to my stomach. I had never, ever thought Zoe would be capable of something like this. I knew she had problems that ran deep, I knew she had seen a lot of darkness in her life. But I never knew she was this messed up.

I started crying as I kept reading. The things she wrote about us. It only got worse. A little for myself, but more for Chris. I didn't care if horse show people thought I was a slut or a bitch, or whatever. But Chris? He had a reputation. This was his career, his living, his everything. He couldn't have this kind of stuff out there.

"I can't believe she would do this," I said to Chris. "I guess I can believe she'd do it to me, but to you . . ."

"I thought she was our friend," Chris said.

I looked at him. What he had just said . . . It meant he believed me. "So you believe it wasn't me?" I said.

Chris reached out. "I knew you wouldn't do something like this . . . but I had no other way of explaining it. And Dale thought it would be better to . . . Now it all makes sense. You were right about Zoe, about her being jealous."

"But still, if you hadn't gotten involved with me . . . this would have never happened."

"True," he said.

I let my eyes fall to the floor. He lifted my chin with his hand.

"I don't regret it," he said.

"Really?"

"How could I?"

He kissed me. Slow and deep. Full of love and emotion and relief. Our feelings flowed between us in the one kiss.

"What are we going to do?" I said, when we'd pulled apart.

"I don't know yet," Chris said.

"So the whole horse show world has—" I stopped myself there.

"Yup, pretty much."

We had sex right there in the kitchen. With me pressed up against the kitchen table, the edge of the table cutting into my thighs. I guess it was make-up sex. It was different than the times before. It was rougher, tinged somehow with what had happened between us. I'm not sure if Chris was angry with me or just angry with what had happened, but I felt his anger in the way he touched me. He tore my shirt over my head and pulled my jeans down, not caring if the denim scraped my skin. He didn't wait for me to take my jeans all the way off and he didn't bother with my bra. He pulled my panties down to meet my jeans, which were stuck at my shins. Then he pushed me, slightly playfully but also somewhat seriously back onto the table. He climbed on top of me and put himself inside me. Not slowly, carefully like he had before, but immediately pushing all the way in. I gulped as I felt him all the way inside me. He held my arms down, not exactly pinning me there, but not letting me up either.

He did ask, "Are you okay?" as he started to thrust into me.

"Yes," I whispered. He would have stopped if I had shown any hesitation and I knew that. I always thought make-up sex was full of passion and feeling, but now I saw it was also still full of anger and turmoil.

He thrust harder, the skin of his abdomen slapping into mine. I wasn't near coming, but it felt pleasurable and exciting in a way I'd never known existed. He groaned and closed his hands tighter on my arms. Would I have bruises tomorrow? Maybe light ones? I didn't care.

He kept thrusting into me, going further inside me than I think I knew existed. It was animalistic, this kind of sex we were having, but in the best sense. In the rawest, most sexy sense. I loved feeling every inch of his taut muscles and looking at his tensed face as he moved over me.

Then he came and shuddered into silence on top of me.

"I'm sorry," he said. His voice was hoarse, as if he'd just been screaming for hours at a concert. That was how it felt—that we'd screamed and thrashed and finally come to a close.

I wasn't sure what he was sorry for. For fucking me like that, or for thinking I'd written those things.

# Chapter 33

THE NEXT MORNING'S LESSON was different from all the rest before it. For one thing Chris and I arrived at the barn together. We were also late. Both were part of our plan.

Chris led Logan into the grooming stall and started brushing him. I opened my trunk and pulled out Logan's bridle, saddle, saddle pad, and girth. When I looked into the grooming stall, Chris was brushing Logan's face and Logan was nuzzling him.

"I guess he likes you," I said.

Chris finished brushing Logan and I handed him the bridle. Every morning since I had been at the horse show, I had always worked alone, brushing Logan, tacking him up. I smiled as I watched Chris; it was nice to have company.

I pulled my helmet and half-chaps from my trunk as Chris did up the girth. He led Logan out of the grooming stall and was halfway down the aisle when he stopped.

He turned back to me. "You know what? How about I hop on him today?"

"Sure. If you want to."

Chris looked big on Logan, but not heavy. He sat lightly, with his weight in his joints, not in his seat. I sat in the middle of the schooling ring on one of the jumps, legs stretched out in front of me.

Chris picked up a trot and I watched him wrap his legs tightly around Logan's sides. His legs never moved. I could tell it wasn't because he was trying hard to keep them still, but because his legs were so strong. At first Chris kept his reins long and frequently he put them in one hand and patted Logan with his other hand. Logan kept his head high in the air as Chris pressed him forward. I began to think that Logan looked part-giraffe.

Chris kept moving Logan forward, making him strut out at the trot. When he began to shorten his reins and take a feel on Logan's mouth, Logan started to chew the bit and raised his head higher. Logan was doing to Chris what he always did to me. I could tell just what Chris was feeling, just what it felt like to ride Logan at that moment, and when Logan threw his head once more vigorously, I was glad to be on the ground watching.

"That's fine," Chris said. "See what he's doing here? Trying to evade me like he does with you. More leg and more hand together and there—" Logan lowered his head slightly. "Keep the leg, keep him forward until he starts to give and then slow things down. That's what you have to learn to do." Chris looked at me. "You have to learn to push, to keep going even if it feels a little uneasy and then you'll get results."

Each time Chris rose out of the saddle and came down

again, it was slow. Soon, Logan's trot was slow too, not a crawl but relaxed and elongated so that he was covering more ground.

"And keep the leg, keep the pressure on at all times so he doesn't decide you've backed off. There. See that? See how he's listening to what I want from him?"

I nodded, but Chris didn't see me, his eyes were focused straight ahead. He sat to the trot and then picked up a canter. "And there again," he said, as Logan softened his back under Chris's weight. Instead of cantering fast and low across the ground, Logan's canter looked like that of a carousel horse, rocking back and forth fluidly. Chris got out of the saddle into his half-seat and pressed Logan forward and then sat down again, collecting his stride.

"He looks great," I said. What he really looked like was a totally different horse. A good one. Maybe I should have felt annoyed that I couldn't get him to go so well. Any other rider and maybe I would have been hurt inside, but I didn't mind because it was Chris. And what horse wouldn't go better for Chris?

"He feels good," Chris said. "How about dropping that vertical?"

I put the jump down and I moved to the side. Chris turned the corner to it, now back at the trot. Chris increased his leg against Logan's side as he approached. Logan hesitated slightly as he reached the jump and Chris sat back in the saddle and legged him. Logan bounded over. On the other side, Chris sat to the trot, forcing Logan forward with his leg. He turned to the vertical again and this time Logan needed less leg.

Chris stopped on the other side, patted Logan, and asked me to raise the jump. He trotted it again, keeping Logan's pace slow but full of impulsion. I could see Logan's eyes studying the jump as he approached it, the bit of white gleaming, letting me know that he was not always sure of himself.

Chris jumped the vertical twice and then halted again.

"He's anxious because he doesn't know what to do when he gets to the jump. He likes to hesitate, or try to run at it. And that's when you get worried. He's looking for the word from you to tell him okay, now jump."

I nodded even though I could barely see the mistakes that he felt.

"Trotting jumps on him is great. It makes him listen and relax. Let's put it up again and see if we can get an even more relaxed jump out of him at a bigger height."

I put the rail up two holes so that it now measured about three-foot-three—about the height I showed over. Chris trotted it back and forth, and then picked up a canter and cantered it twice. He kept cantering and said, "Can you go up two more, please."

I put the rail up and Chris cantered it again. Logan sailed over it with ease.

Chris turned to the other jump in the ring—an oxer that was already set up. Logan jumped it no problem.

"Put the oxer up a couple," Chris said. "Let's surprise him a little and see what he can do."

The jump was almost up to my ribs and measured about four feet high. It wasn't big for Chris, but it was the highest Logan had ever jumped, as far as I knew.

Chris cantered the jump perfectly. Logan jumped it so effortlessly that I squinted at him, wondering if he was really my horse.

Chris grinned at me. "Wanna go up a few more?"

The jump was four-foot-three. Logan jumped it clear by at least six inches. Chris halted on the other side and patted him. Logan sighed and lowered his head.

"You know, you don't have a bad horse here," he said.

Great, after everything, my dad had picked a winner, a diamond in the rough. His impressive reach extended beyond the business world to nearly anything he touched, even a sport he knew nothing about. It's not that I wanted Logan to be worthless, but did he have to be awesome?

"Yeah, when you're on him," I said.

Chris walked Logan into the center of the ring and halted in front of me.

"Do you think he could really be a decent jumper, like a grand prix jumper?" A plan was forming in my head.

"I don't know about grand prix, but he's definitely got some scope."

Chris swung his leg over the saddle and dismounted, landing close to me, as I stood by Logan's head. Chris took off his helmet and wiped his forehead with his arm. He leaned close and kissed me. We weren't sneaking around anymore.

* * *

So that was how we played it. Starting that morning and for the rest of the circuit, we were a couple. We hung out together around the show, we held hands, we even kissed in public. If I had really written A SUMMER OF HORSE SHOW FIRSTS, would

Chris Kern still be with me? No, was the answer anyone with half a brain would come to on their own. On *The Chronicle* bulletin boards, Chris posted a plea to whoever was out there to leave us alone. *There have been some hurtful things written online about my girlfriend, Hannah, and me. I wish no ill will toward the person who wrote these things. I feel sorry for whoever it is. I'm sure some people will continue to try to slander us in public for reasons I also can't understand. But please, if you can, respect our privacy.*

Of course there was the matter of Jamie. If she hadn't read it yet, she would likely read it soon. Or hear about it. She probably already had. She would go to my parents, so I had to go to them first.

I started with my dad. "I have a plan and it's not just for the fall—it starts today," I told him when I finally caught him in between meetings.

"Okay, pitch me."

I could hear the rustling of papers. He wasn't giving me his full attention but I had no choice but to take this opportunity to convince him of my plan. I couldn't wait any longer. For all I knew, Jamie had already called Mom and was scaring the crap out of her, causing her anxiety to flare to all-new levels. It wouldn't take much to spin Chris into some kind of pervy predator.

"I lied to you," I told my dad. "I haven't gotten better—Logan and I—haven't gotten better because of Jamie. I've been having lessons every morning with Chris Kern. He's a grand prix rider, you can google him and look up everything he's won—it's impressive. Even you will be impressed. He's also my boyfriend, but that happened after he started helping me. Jamie's the worst trainer. She doesn't invest any time in Logan or me. Chris knows how to teach and he knows talent when he sees it. I'm not talking about me here. I can ride better but let's not kid ourselves—I'm not some great rider. But Chris sees a lot of potential in Logan. You were right— he's a super talented horse."

I could imagine my dad's expression as he took this in. Some of it he might not love—the boyfriend part, for sure. He'd feel protective of me. Although maybe that was part of sending me away for the summer. Not just making me learn to take care of Logan and survive on my own, but maybe, he even wanted me to live a little. To get out of Mom's suffocating bird-crazy world. Either way, I knew he would love hearing that Logan was talented. That he had handpicked a good horse. I was playing to his ego, something that never failed to appeal to him. And I was right—the rustling stopped. I had his full attention now.

"Chris rode him the other day and you should have seen them. He jumped 1.30 meters and it looked like Logan wasn't even trying. Chris isn't saying Logan is going to the Olympics, but there's undiscovered talent there." I had planned out that last phrase—undiscovered talent. And I threw out another zinger: "Logan has untapped market potential."

"Okay," Dad said. "What's your vision plan?"

"The rest of the circuit I train with Chris. We pull out of Jamie's barn completely. Then when the circuit ends, Logan gets on the trailer to go home to Chris's barn in Pennsylvania. He spends the fall working with him, assessing his true potential. I'll be so busy at school I won't have time to ride anyway, like you said. Then we reevaluate. Chris will tell us honestly whether Logan has the possibility to be a top horse. If you were right and he really is a special horse, maybe you keep him and see what he and Chris can do together. If not, we sell him."

"And you're okay with that? If I sell him?"

"I trust you'll make the right decision." What I didn't tell my dad was my other part of the plan—if Logan went well and we kept him, maybe I could commute down to Florida on weekends to show him. And to see Chris.

What I also was secretly harboring in my mind was that even if Logan didn't end up having the talent to be a top horse, perhaps Chris and my dad would hit it off. Hopefully my dad would see Chris's talent, his drive, his devotion, and maybe he'd decide to buy another horse for Chris. I could suggest my father and I meet Chris at a show or two this fall so my dad could see Chris ride and get to know him better.

Dad was silent. I waited, pressing my eyes closed and hoping so hard he'd be impressed by my plan.

Finally, he said, "Good for you, Hannah. Good for you. I knew this summer would be just what you needed."

I smiled, letting my dad think that sending me off to Vermont without a groom, all on my own, was what had taught me so much. And it had taught me a lot. But being with Chris had taught me much more about who I was.

He continued, "I need to do a little due diligence on Chris. It shouldn't take long. I'll call you back with my decision."

His words sounded slightly spooky, like he had spies

ready and waiting to find out about anyone he needed info on. Did he have a P.I. on the payroll?

"What about Mom? I'm worried Jamie might already be getting in touch with her. Some people wrote things on the internet about Chris and me." I shuddered, thinking of my dad possibly reading A SUMMER OF HORSE SHOW FIRSTS. How had I not thought this part through?

"Why would they do that?" he asked.

"They're jealous, I guess," I said.

"Okay. Is there anything else you need to tell me?"

"Chris is older than me. He's twenty-three."

"Yes, I see that."

Apparently he was already googling Chris Kern.

"Dad—" I said.

"I'll be back in touch with my decision," he said and hung up.

My dad would be back in touch with his decision. His decision about Logan, I reminded myself. He couldn't make a decision about me being with Chris. That was my decision to make and not one that he could force upon me. Or could he?

# Chapter 34

IT STARTED RAINING THAT NIGHT and didn't stop. It was the kind of rain that comes in the mountains, hard slapping sheets that welled up into huge puddles all over the show grounds. By midday the rings were under an inch of water and classes were temporarily postponed. At two o'clock, it was announced that classes were canceled for the day and that tomorrow's events were still up in the air.

It kept raining throughout the night. I slept at Chris's, waking frequently to the sound of thunder and wondered whether Logan was scared. Jasper had climbed into bed with us, shivering under the covers. In the morning it was still pouring. I wore a baseball hat and my raincoat to the barn but by the time I had run to the tent, my hat was soaked and my raincoat leaking.

Classes were called off again and everybody at the horse show spent the day under their respective tents, working on making their barn as flood-proof as possible. It was hard not to feel isolated as I worked to secure my area. I could hear

Zoe a few aisles over, calling to the grooms and Jamie. "Let's put the hay in here for now and move the grain, okay?"

MISSION came on and I heard someone yell, "Turn it up!"

Chris helped me when he could, which made things a little better. I dug a six-inch trench all around the aisle to keep the water out and covered the hay and grain with extra tarps that Chris had. The trench was pretty much full with water a half an hour after I had finished it. I looked out at the show grounds, covered in water and mud—I didn't know where the rain, which kept pouring down with no sign of relenting, would go.

The rest of the day, I spent waiting. I groomed Logan three times even though he was already clean. By two o'clock, the rings looked like swimming pools and it was hard to imagine that they would ever dry up. People were claiming it was the worst the show had ever been hit and the most classes ever canceled. Some people were even considering leaving before the water started seeping in on the horses.

Then, finally, the rain stopped. It didn't come to an end slowly, but went from pouring to clear. The sun came out for the first time in days and it was amazing how quickly the show grounds dried up. At first glance, the flooded rings seemed like they would never return to their previous state, but by the end of the day there was only a thin film of water covering them and by the next morning, they were practically dry. It was announced that classes would resume.

\* \* \*

I trembled slightly as I put my foot in the stirrup and mounted Logan. I had lunged him that morning, making sure that all his extra energy, compiled while waiting for the storm to pass, was cantered out. Still, I could tell by the way he wiggled while I tightened the girth that he felt excited to be outside again.

On the way up to the ring, I rehearsed in my head what I would say to Jamie. Chris and I were working on getting him to listen . . . I think it would be best to school him over a lot of low fences to get his attention . . . what I think we should do . . .

None of it seemed right. I didn't see how I could even pretend to handle the situation delicately or maturely. I kept thinking about what all the people at the show might be saying about me. But I had to try to put that out of my mind. When I saw Jamie, and Zoe next to her, my mouth went dry. Jamie turned from the in-gate to face me. I noticed lines in her face I'd never seen before, deep creases in sun-browned flesh.

"Good morning," Jamie said in a monotone.

My stomach tightened. "Good morning."

"The course is pretty straight forward. I'll go check where you are in the order and let Zoe go over it with you."

I tried to swallow but my throat felt like pebbles. I wished I could say something, anything, to keep Jamie from walking away, from leaving me alone with Zoe. Did Jamie know about everything with Zoe and was she doing this to make me suffer more?

"The course is as follows—" Zoe flipped her hair back with her good arm.

"The gate on the far side, the line through the diagonal, the oxer in the corner . . ."

I listened as Zoe droned on in her white shorts and baby

blue polo, her arm still in its sling. Only a few weeks before I had thought Zoe was my friend. A friend like I'd never had in high school. A friend I'd talk about to people I met at college. Like, oh once my friend Zoe said . . . or once Zoe and I . . .

It wasn't that we'd ever had that much in common. We lived such different lives, but it hadn't seemed to matter. But now that was all gone.

I couldn't just sit there and listen to Zoe without saying anything about what she'd done. "Just stop," I told her. "I know what you did."

Just then, Jamie returned, "Let's go, you're in ten. Got the course down?"

Out in the schooling ring, Jamie didn't say much. I tried to remember if Jamie had ever said a lot to me. I decided that she hadn't, but that somehow her lack of words before had seemed very different. Like she didn't know where to start, so much was wrong. Now it seemed like her silence was calculated, taking revenge on me.

I tried to work by myself inside the silence. I had discussed with Chris how to handle Logan after the rain. How to demand his attention slowly, starting by asking him to go forward and then shorten. Then to progress to bending him around the corners, and then to practice transitions from the trot to the canter to the trot, all the time half-halting. I tried to immerse myself within my ride, concentrating solely on Logan's responses to my aids.

When I was at the in-gate waiting to go, I watched the rider before me and made sure I knew the course. Jamie was standing next to me, and Zoe on the other side of Jamie. I spotted Chris across the ring, filming me on his iPhone. I had asked him to, so if Logan went well we could send the video to my dad as evidence of why I should move to Chris's barn. When Philip said, "Hannah, you're in," I took a deep breath and squeezed Logan forward.

Instead of hesitating upon entering, I departed directly into a canter. I cantered down the long side of ring, brought Logan back to a walk (test that he's listening to you, Chris had said), waited for the tone and then departed into a canter again. As I approached the first fence, I felt more secure in my position than ever. Instead of the days of not riding and Jamie's and Zoe's glare making me looser, I felt tight and in control. Maybe it was the extra sticky spray I'd used or maybe I was getting stronger like Chris had said I would. Either way, I would show them how good I could be.

"Ride every point of the course," Chris had said. "Ride the corners, that's your chance to check Logan, to make sure he's listening to you."

I flowed around the course. Not effortlessly, although it may have looked rather smooth. Instead, each stride was an exact movement that I measured with my muscles. We had no rails down and finished within the time-allowed. The jump-off was straightforward, with the only time to cut seconds a long approach to a single vertical. What would Chris have me do? Gallop it full force? Play it safe and not worry about my time?

I didn't look to Jamie for any answers. Instead when the tone went off, I cantered the first four jumps of the jump-off in much the same manner that I had jumped the first course.

When I landed off the fourth jump and headed to the fifth, the long approach, I squeezed Logan forward while still keeping a feel on the reins. If I threw him away, he would be likely to take off and scamper to the fence. I needed to keep him listening while pressing him forward. Five strides away from the fence, I eased down into the saddle. I half-halted Logan and sailed over the fence.

"A clean go and a time of 44.98 in the jump-off for Personal Best and Hannah Waer."

Jamie and Zoe acted like I hadn't just ridden the round of my life.

"Good job," Jamie said. Zoe said nothing; she wouldn't meet my eyes. That was fine. They could play their own mind games if they wanted.

Back at the barn, Chris was waiting. "Great ride. Perfectly executed." He passed me his phone. "Do you want to see for yourself?"

We watched the video together. Chris was right. It did look good. I was amazed at how in control Logan looked. And how happy he looked. His ears were pricked forward the whole way around the course. He liked his job now.

"Forward it to me and I'll send it to my dad," I told him.

I did just that, and then we waited.

# Chapter 35

MY DAD FINALLY CALLED. He didn't start with some casual normal conversation opener like, "Hi," or "How's everything?" He just said, "Okay."

"Okay what?" I said, even though I was pretty sure I knew what he was okaying.

"Okay, you can move barns and send Logan home with Chris. He'll have two months with him and then we'll re-assess. But there's one condition."

Of course there was. Nothing was ever straight-forward-you-can-have-what-you-want with my dad. He spent too much time managing business transactions that always included this assumption and that agreement.

"You will be the one informing Jamie," Dad said.

I swallowed hard. I had to tell her I was leaving her barn? Would she even care, or would she be glad to be rid of me? I had to imagine she was the type of person who would make things ugly for clients who left. She didn't seem like the type of trainer to take the high road and be professional. She probably preferred being the dumper, not the dumpee.

"Don't you think she won't believe me or something?" I said to Dad. "I mean, isn't it weird for me to do it?"

"Do you know when I fired my first employee?" he asked.

I wanted to say, "When you were thirteen?" but I bit my tongue. He was giving me what I wanted, after all. "No," I said. "I don't."

"I was eighteen. Your age. Ryan has had to fire plenty of people. It's an important skill and I want you to learn it."

"Okay," I said. "If that's what you want, I'll do it."

I had no idea how, but if it meant riding with Chris instead of Jamie, I'd do it.

* * *

I think I was the only eighteen-year-old in the history of horse shows who ever had to fire her trainer. Well, in the history of horse shows in the twenty-first century anyway. Most parents paid the bills, made the decisions, and had the difficult conversations. Cheryl called her mother nearly every day to report on how she'd done and by all accounts she was a full-on grown-up. I'd heard Cheryl talking to her mom about paying a credit card bill—apparently her mom footed the bill for not just her horse show life, but for the rest of her life too. "How am I going to do it?" I asked Chris.

"It's a tough one. I guess just be honest with her."

One of the things I loved perhaps most about that summer was the two different Chris Kerns I got to see. Of course they weren't actually different. But there was the grand prix rider, who wore Pikeur breeches and Parlanti boots and shirt and coat and helmet. He looked incredibly hot in his show clothes—professional and radiating a star-like quality. He was one of the most well known riders in the entire country and I loved watching him ride and then get off and take off his helmet, his hair slightly sweaty underneath. I loved how he would put his helmet in the crook of his arm and with his other hand wipe the sweat from his forehead.

Then there was the other Chris, the Chris when we weren't at the horse show. The Chris standing before me right then, making me dinner. The regular guy Chris, who was still smoking hot. The Chris in perfectly fitting jeans, loafers, and a button-down shirt. When I saw that Chris, my breathing stuttered for a second. He had totally transformed. I guess maybe it was like dating a professional baseball player or a police officer. You got two for the price of one—you got to stand in awe and lust after the man in the uniform and then again when you saw him in regular street clothes.

I said, "So tell her she's a terrible trainer and she treated me like dirt and she's fired?"

Chris poured a little olive oil into the pan on the stove. "Okay, maybe not *that* honest."

"What do you think she'll be like? You know her better than I do."

"Well, Jamie's the type who does things that don't make sense. Like, she's the type to get pissed when a trouble client leaves her."

"So I'm a trouble client?" I walked over and put my arms around him.

"I didn't mean you."

"Now I'm *your* trouble client," I said, moving my hands to his belt. "You're going to have to make me happy and it might not be easy."

"I think I can handle it," he said, putting his arms around my waist.

"Oh yeah?"

He kissed me, slow like he was trying to tempt me. "I think I know what you want."

"I'll be the judge of that," I said.

But Chris did know what I wanted. He made it all about me right then, about my pleasure. We went into the bedroom, he laid me down on the bed, slowly took off all my clothes. When he touched me it became all about the pressure. At first it was slow and light, barely grazing my skin, making me arch my back and yearn for more. Then it was more direct and deliberate, but still not too much or too hard. My breathing quickened and I gave in to thinking about nothing but myself. For the first time ever, I was vocal, gasping at first and then moaning as he glided his fingers back and forth over and then inside me. Somehow he knew to gradually touch me stronger and deeper until I came. Afterwards he was smiling, clearly pleased with his talents. And he was hard—something I had wondered about as he was touching me. Very hard. We so weren't done.

\* \* \*

I decided to tell Jamie as she was making up the next day's schedule in the tack room. Of course Zoe was there.

"Hi, Jamie, can I talk to you?" I asked.

Jamie didn't turn from the whiteboard. "Do you think we should school Ranger before the A/Os or just flat him?" she asked Zoe.

Had she heard me? Or was this selective hearing? I asked her louder if I could talk to her.

"Yes, what?"

I glanced at Zoe. "I was sort of thinking maybe in private?"

"I don't have all day," Jamie said. "Say what you've got to say."

So I had to do this in front of Zoe. Perfect.

"I'm moving Logan. Well, not actually moving him now. I'm keeping him at my stalls, but I'm changing trainers . . . to Chris. And Logan's going home with Chris to Pennsylvania after Circuit."

For the first time Jamie turned to look at me.

I continued, "I want to thank you for everything you've done for me. But it's time for a change for us."

"So you want me to believe your mom and dad are letting you move your horse to the barn of the guy you're fucking?" she said.

"It's not just . . . this isn't about—" Her coarseness left me stumbling for words. I guess I had assumed she'd be angry, but I hadn't thought she'd go that low.

"Everyone read your little diary. Do your mom and dad know about that?"

"I didn't write that stuff." I stared hard at Zoe. "Someone who was jealous of me and Chris did." I took a deep breath. I would be professional. I wouldn't stoop to Jamie's level. I tried to channel my father. "I think we're getting off track. I came to tell you my plans, which my parents are in agreement with."

"Flat or school?" Jamie turned back to the whiteboard, making it clear she was done with me. She'd probably never speak to me again.

"School," Zoe said.

"What about Harley? I think he could use a lunge."

I stood there a moment longer. Chris had warned me that Jamie would be like this. It shouldn't have hurt as much as it did. And what did I expect from Zoe? For her to take my side, or give me any signal of regret for what she had written? No, that wasn't going to happen.

# Chapter 36

WE SPENT THE EVENING on Chris's couch, watching more HOUSE OF CARDS. Half the horse show was probably at Backcountry and maybe we should have gone out together too, to make a statement, but we'd decided to stay in. I had planned to call my roommate-to-be, but I kept putting it off. Now it was almost getting too late to call.

"Oh, come on. You've been sitting there with your phone in your hand for the whole night," Chris said.

I had filled out the online questionnaire from Tufts back in the early summer, before coming to Vermont. Early to bed—check. Early to rise—check. Neat and tidy—check. I guess I was still all those same things, but somehow I felt that if given the chance to fill out the form now I'd do it differently. I was a different person and I no longer wanted the boring, dorky roommate I had imagined back in June.

I dialed the number. Her phone had one of those enjoy-this-music-while-you-wait things: a song I'd never heard before. I'd tried connecting with Elizabeth Van Norman of

Tucson, Arizona via Facebook but she'd ignored my friend-requests. What did it say when your future roommate didn't want to be your Facebook friend?

Finally, she answered, "Yeah?"

"Hi, is this Elizabeth?"

"Who wants to know?"

"Um, it's Hannah Waer. I'm going to be your . . . we're going to be roommates . . . at Tufts?"

I covered the phone and mouthed "help" at Chris, who motioned to me with a flick of his hand to keep talking to her.

"Oh yeah, it's just . . . no one calls me Elizabeth. It's Van."

"Oh, cool."

Somehow Van didn't seem like someone who was early to bed early to rise. Van with a strange song I'd never heard didn't seem like someone who would make her bed and bring a vacuum with her to school (I was most definitely bringing my stick-vacuum).

"So you're from . . . I forget?" Van asked.

"I'm from Boston."

"Hometown girl, huh?"

"Yeah, kind of lame, I know."

"Whatever. So, like, I don't really sleep at night."

"You mean you go to bed late?"

"No, like I don't sleep. I'm not like part of the Cullen coven or anything but I usually just nap a few hours during the day."

"But this . . . I mean did you fill out the form?"

"Form?"

"We all got a form, over email? About whether we go to bed early or like a neat room?"

"Oh shit. I'm sure my mom filled that out. She hacks into my email all the time." Van laughed. "Poor you. She probably made me sound all perfect, like I study all the time and like to organize my sock drawer in my free time."

I joined her in laughing a little. What else was there to do? And in a way I was kind of relieved. I wasn't getting some clone of me to live with. I'm not sure it would exactly work out to have a roommate who kept a vampire schedule, but at least I wouldn't be living with my long-lost type A twin.

When I got off the phone, Chris looked at me with curious eyes.

I told him about the mix-up and he said I could probably petition to get a new roommate before school even started.

I shrugged off his idea. "Something tells me to wing it. I never thought coming here this summer and taking care of Logan by myself would work out and it did. I need to learn to be more go-with-the-flow."

"I guess that's a great attitude," he said, like he still thought I was planning my own funeral.

"She asked if I had a boyfriend. She dates someone in a band and he plays gigs in Boston."

"And do you?" he said, his eyes curious again.

I smiled shyly. "I said yes. Was that right?"

Chris moved closer and put his face inches from mine. "Sounds right to me."

He kissed me and I had to pull away to ask, "What's going to happen? I mean when Circuit's over?" I had put this convo off for too long.

Chris tilted his head to one side. "You could come to some of the shows, especially since I'll have Logan."

"And maybe you could come visit me at school?" I wished I'd said, come visit me in Boston. Why would Chris want to come to my dorm room? No, we'd stay at a nice hotel. Have breakfast in bed. I couldn't possibly imagine him in a dorm room, crammed into a twin size bed with me. Suddenly I felt so much younger than him and I wished life were different and we were the same age and things like this wouldn't be a problem. "You're not going to want to come visit me at school. I mean, how could you even, with your show schedule."

"I don't know," he said. "We'll have to see what my schedule is like by then."

"What do you mean? Don't you already know?"

Top riders always had their show schedules planned out for the entire year. Changes might come up, like how he'd come to Vermont instead of going to Europe, sure, but there was a plan in place. His entries for fall shows would already have to be in.

"So she's not very neat?" he said, trying to turn the conversation back to Van. It was clear he was avoiding something.

"What's going on?" I said. "What shows are you doing this fall?" Maybe he was going to Europe for the fall, or maybe he'd decided to move there.

"I don't quite know yet," he said again.

"What aren't you telling me?" I put my hand on his arm. "You need to tell me."

He finally looked at me, and his eyes were sad. He was trying to fight it, but they were sad. "Harris is pulling his horses. This is my last show with them."

"What? Why?" I let go of his arm.

"A lot of reasons."

"Do you think Alexa told him to because you didn't, *you know*?"

"Possibly."

"What did he say? What reason did he give?"

Chris gave me a look that said, *you don't want to know.*

"Because of the stuff online?" I said.

He nodded slowly like he didn't want to hurt me.

"So it was because of me?" I leaned back on the couch.

"Maybe a little, but not only. I wasn't exactly killing it with his horses."

"Does he know where he's taking them?"

"Of course."

I felt dumb that I'd thought Harris would just leave Chris without a plan. This was a high-stakes business and sometimes I lost sight of that. Smart owners didn't make hasty decisions without a thought-out plan.

"He's giving the rides to Tommy."

"So what are you going to do?" I hung my head. Chris had lost his rides. Even worse, the horses were going to one of Chris's *friends.* "This is all because of me. I've ruined your reputation. How are you ever going to get grand prix horses again?"

Chris put his arm around me. "This is not all because of you, and my reputation is not ruined. Things will blow over. People forget things and this will be a blip in the road. You know Keith? He was sued for cheating his owners out of money five years ago. He had a lean year or two where everyone left him and now he's turning clients away, his barn is so full. And remember, I wasn't so happy with Harris anyway."

"Yeah, but you weren't ready to dump him. Now you have *no* horses."

"I have Logan."

"Yeah, Logan, awesome."

"And Arkos. I'm buying Harris out."

I felt a little hurt that this had all happened without me knowing. That Chris had gone through this alone, or rather with Dale. It felt weird, but I was jealous of Dale. His advice and counsel was more important than mine. Stop—I told myself. Dale had known Chris forever. And he knew the horse world. I had only known Chris just over a month and I didn't know the first thing about the politics of show jumping. And Chris was also just trying to protect my feelings. Still, my jealously didn't fade completely.

I said in a defeated tone, "Arkos and Logan."

Chris sounded upbeat as he repeated, "Arkos and Logan. This is going to be fine. This is going to be better in the end. Okay?"

"Okay," I said, but I wasn't sure I believed him.

# Chapter 37

THERE WAS A CLASSIC NEARLY every week for the high children's jumpers, but I hadn't ever come close to getting around the course clean and being competitive. I thought I had a slim chance of going clean so I went to the tack store and bought a pair of white breeches. I'd always admired the white breeches girls wore around the show on classic days. Maybe *admired* was too weak a verb. More like *coveted*. I'd never thought it made much sense for me, though, and it probably still didn't even if I had a chance of making it into the jump-off. White breeches weren't required and who knew when I'd wear them again? It was unclear whether I'd show again after Vermont.

Yet, there was something so cool about wearing white at a horse show, the color most likely to get dirty at the place most likely to be full of dirt. I felt like my legs were glowing. I felt so entirely good about myself as I walked around the show grounds the morning of the classic that they were worth the price tag. Of course I hadn't jumped a single jump and I wouldn't feel so good if I was soon lying in a pile of dirt, having been dumped by Logan.

Before I got on Logan, I stood in front of the tent and surveyed the horse show. Grooms were leading horses to the rings, trainers were shooting by in their golf carts, dogs barked from their positions tied to the tents. I was going to miss all this. It was like its own little world and I'd come to know nearly everybody, from Stacy who worked at the food truck, to Janet and Hank who owned the mobile tack store, to Jeff, who delivered the feed. I knew every rider in the grand prix now, since each week many of the same riders competed. I knew how they had done the week before, whether they had placed, which horse had gone well. It was hard to imagine that in a week all this would disappear—the people, the horses, the tents. All that would be left until next year were the empty fields with dead grass from where the tents had been. And the people and the horses would go on to other shows down the road, Chris included. Without me, of course.

I spent so long learning the course I could see it with my eyes closed. It was trickier than the usual ones. You had to know where to be smart and where to risk things—I thought to myself. I was starting to sound like Chris. The main trap came on the home stretch, a large oxer in the corner. It wasn't the height, but it was the location of the jump, only about ten strides after the triple combination. If you made it clear through the triple, you would have the oxer to contend with. I knew I would have to balance up quickly after the combination. If I let Logan pull me to the oxer, I would probably meet it strung out and have it down.

The order for the classic was drawn randomly. I was slated to go fourteenth of thirty-six. It was a good draw, early enough so I wouldn't sit around getting nervous, but late enough to be able to watch a few ride the course.

I loved walking the course with Chris, in my white breeches no less. Chris focused on me in a way that Jamie never had. He took into consideration every turn and every jump, and we talked about how to ride everything. I could feel other people looking at us. Maybe they were thinking about A SUMMER OF HORSE SHOW FIRSTS, but I felt more like they were looking at us in awe, knowing I was Chris Kern's girlfriend. It felt nearly unbelievable to me in a way, too. I had come to Vermont hardly knowing who Chris was and now he was my boyfriend. But for how much longer?

We watched the first few horses to see how the course rode. Chris was right about the oxer taking its toll. A few other riders had parts of the triple down. Logan warmed up well and I felt as good as I could when I stood at the in-gate waiting for the horse before me to finish up. I didn't know why, but something made me look down the side of the ring. I wished I hadn't because I saw Jamie standing there, watching. She didn't have any reason to be at the ring. I had been her only children's jumper rider. She was clearly there to watch me. To make me feel uncomfortable, to put the pressure on. She would want nothing more than to see me fail. That would be the ultimate revenge for her.

I decided not to tell Chris I saw her. I didn't want to make a bigger deal of it than it already felt like it was. I wouldn't give her the power she wanted. I rode into the ring at a trot. I halted Logan when I was halfway down the long side and backed him a few steps to make him pay attention. When the signal sounded, I picked up a canter. The first three jumps were singles. I rode them accurately. The first round of the classic was comparable to the first round of a regular class. The idea was to have no jumping faults and stay within the time-allowed. Then, in the jump-off, speed as well as fallen rails would determine the winner. But I wasn't even thinking about the jump-off. All I was thinking about was riding my best over this course. I would be thrilled if I rode well, even if I ended up having a rail or two. Chris had told me not to worry about the time-allowed. He said it wasn't particularly tight and he'd rather have me leave the jumps up and have a time fault at this point. He also said Logan was a naturally quick horse so it probably wouldn't be an issue for him anyway.

I rode through a bending line across the diagonal and then to the triple combination. The triple worked out well, Logan jumping up high, yet remaining calm. When I landed off the last effort of the triple, I sat back in the saddle. The oxer was next. I had actually been clean so far. Suddenly my brain switched from just wanting to survive and get around the course to wanting to go clear. My competitive side kicked in and I began thinking about making it into the jump-off. What would Jamie think if I went clean and made it into the jump-off? I wasn't sure how my time was, but I couldn't worry about that now. Even going clean with time faults would feel like a big win, although now I wanted to go totally clean.

For three strides I steadied Logan. I could feel him tugging on the bit, wanting to surge forward toward the next jump. I half-halted him hard—once and once again. When I felt him respond and slow down, I loosened my arms. The jump was only a few strides away. I relaxed my back and legged Logan lightly. He sailed over the jump perfectly.

Only one jump left, I said to myself as I landed from the oxer. It was a plain vertical with a panel that said EQUIFIT across it. I steadied Logan once more, and softly said, "whoa." We met the jump at what seemed like a perfect distance. I got up into jumping position, releasing with my hands to give Logan his head. As I was halfway over the fence, I heard Logan hit it with his back hooves. The pole rattled in the cups. Had it come down?

I waited for the announcer to say, "Four faults." And what about my time?

Before I could look behind me to see if the jump was still up, the announcer said, "And that's a clear round for Personal Best and Hannah Waer. No faults and a time of 71.64 seconds, well within the time-allowed."

I looked back at the jump and felt a surge of gratefulness to the show jumping gods above. I couldn't believe it had stayed up. I patted Logan on the neck and exited the ring.

"I got a little lucky," I said to Chris. I leaned forward onto Logan's neck, so I was at Chris's eye level. I couldn't stop smiling. I was clear. I was clear! I was going into the jump-off and the cherry on top was that Jamie had seen it all.

Chris said, "You need to watch your back in the air. You snapped open too early from your release. It caught Logan off guard, made him nab it with his back shoes. Let the horse worry about the front rails, the rider's job is to worry about the back rails."

"What does that mean?"

"Just that your horse's job is to jump up well enough with his front end and clear the jump coming in; your job is to make sure he gets over the fence well enough to not have the rail down behind."

I nodded. "And I didn't do my job. He did his, but I caught him in the air."

"It was a great ride, Hannah," Chris said. "You're thinking about landing and regrouping, which is super."

"So I just need to stay forward more on landing?"

"Not really stay forward per se, you just can't snap back like this—" Chris showed me from the ground, how I popped open too quickly with my upper body on landing. "You need to be slower, like this—"

"Okay," I said.

"Do you know your jump-off?"

We had walked the jump-off, but at that point I had been concentrating on the first round.

"I better go learn it again," I said.

# Chapter 38

ONLY SIX HORSES WERE CLEAR, so going into the jump-off I knew I would at least be guaranteed a green ribbon. But shooting for sixth seemed like a pathetic thing to do. What did I have to lose? I was going to ride the best I could and hopefully I would come away with a primary colored ribbon.

I had plenty of time to learn the jump-off course. I went over it in my head again and again, and Chris talked it through with me. It was only seven fences. It started over a broken line where Chris said I should go forward and do five strides, not the conservative six. Then came two tight roll-back turns to a vertical and then an oxer. Another fairly tight turn to a combination, and a long gallop home to a vertical. Chris said the few tight turns in the middle of the course would help me regroup Logan and that I should just worry about making neat turns, not trying to go fast there. He also said I shouldn't race through the combination. He explained that not all parts of a jump-off were meant to be ridden at break-neck speed; you had to be smart and figure out where you could make up some time and where you had to concentrate on clearing the jumps. He said that sometimes since the jumps were so low in the children's jumpers people got away with bad riding where they tore around all the parts of the jump-off and the horses managed to leave the jumps up. But he said they weren't learning how to ride a jump-off the right way and that at the bigger heights they wouldn't get away with that. He also said that kind of riding was plain dangerous at any height. He'd rather have me ride smart and finish lower in the ribbons.

"You can't get away with that kind of riding when you're doing the 1.30 meter classes," he said.

"Like I'd ever be doing 1.30 meters."

"Never say never. And just because you're galloping you don't throw your horse away," Chris said. "Keep a feel on his mouth the whole time, just like I taught you when we first started working together."

We came back in the order we had gone in the first round. Three riders went before me and all had gone clear. I entered the ring at the trot. I halted Logan on the far side and waited for the signal to begin. When I heard the tone, I departed into a canter. I had planned my entrance so I would have practically one whole lap around the ring to build up a little speed for the first jump. As I turned the corner to the fence, Chris yelled, "Go! More pace!"

I had thought I was going fast—but apparently it just felt that way. I pushed Logan forward. There was a certain freedom that came with galloping faster than I ever had voluntarily. Instead of feeling wary of letting go anymore, worried about going any faster than I could handle, I felt exhilarated.

I kept contact with his mouth, though, as I galloped the first fence in stride. I did the five strides as planned. In the air over the second fence, I turned my head to look at the next jump. I would need to make a complete U-turn, but angling the turn back so my next turn would be even sharper. I felt Logan slip out on the bend of the turn. I used my outside leg to guide him over the next jump, and back to the oxer. After the oxer, I pressed Logan forward again as I cut across the ring to the combination on the far side. I approached the combination on a bit of an angle and had to try to ride straight through it and then turn, so Logan would know where he was going. I landed from the combination and kicked.

"Go!" Chris shouted again.

I once again felt the thrill of pressing Logan forward. I saw a long distance and decided to go for it, hoping I wasn't asking Logan for too much. I prayed he didn't chip, or worse, stop. Even if he just jumped too flat and had the rail down that would be okay. I used my leg and put all my trust in Logan to jump from what was a really long distance. He took off and I could see his front legs splayed out in front like he was Superman. Somehow, maybe because of all the scope Chris said he had, he cleared the jump.

I kept pressing him since the timers were still a few strides away. Then I brought Logan to a walk, leaning over to pat his neck, and huffing loudly myself.

"Our third clear round and right to the top of the class for

Personal Best and Hannah Waer with a time of 38.14. That's our fastest so far with two more to go."

I came out of the ring beaming. I had ridden well. I had gone clear. And I had actually been relatively fast!

Taylor Lentz went after me. She was only twelve, and she was a really good rider. She was finishing up on ponies and was definitely going to be one of the top junior riders in the coming years. This would likely be her last year in the children's. She went clear with a time of 37.97, moving into first place. The last to go was Vivian Martin. She was also a consistent winner in the children's jumpers, but unlike Taylor she rode too fast. She was the poster child for what Chris had warned me against—going dangerously all out over every part of the course, not paying attention to how each test of the course was supposed to be ridden. She had a small horse, maybe he was only 15.2 or 15.3, but he was fast and usually jumped clean no matter what distance she got him to.

Today was no different as she attacked the first jump at a mad-gallop, her trainer yelling at her from the in-gate to go even faster. She tore around over the fences, flapping in the saddle, and herking and jerking, kicking her little horse. She found a flyer into the combination and any other horse would have crashed through the second element but her horse somehow managed to pop in a little stride and clear the oxer. As she rode to the last jump, I wished she'd have a rail so badly. It didn't seem fair that this kind of riding would win the class. But that was the thing about the horse shows—like life, they weren't always fair. Sometimes the good riders won. Sometimes the riders who worked the hardest got the blue ribbon and those were the days that felt the best. But sometimes the person who could buy the best horse, or who cared more about winning than the horse's welfare, came home with the top prize. There was no changing that.

Vivian galloped the last jump and cleared it. She was four whole seconds faster than Taylor. No matter what Taylor or I could have done, we wouldn't have beaten her. And that was fine with me. I imagined it was fine with Taylor too.

Back in the ring for the presentation, I thought of how I had once asked Chris what winning a big class was like. Even though I hadn't won, I thought I might feel a little bit of what it was like. Waiting in line as they announced the winner, I replayed my jump-off course in my head, feeling the rhythm of Logan's stride as we jumped.

"And third place in our $15,000 Children's/Adult Jumper Classic is Personal Best, ridden today by Hannah Waer of Hingham, Massachusetts."

The yellow ribbon looked pretty against Logan's bay coat. I also got a check that I slipped into my coat pocket.

The small crowd that was watching clapped, but I only cared about Chris, who was by the in-gate. Maybe Jamie was watching. Probably not. She only wanted to see me fail. Still, she'd hear how well I'd done.

On the walk back to my stalls I saw Jed on his junior hunter. I planned to look away and just keep walking, pretending not to notice him, but he motioned to me to wait for him. When he reached me, he said, "Congrats, wow!"

I waited for him to make some joke—from zero to hero or something like that. Instead he said, "I'm sorry I couldn't tell you."

"Loyalty first, I guess I get it," I said.

"If you understand then you're a pretty amazing person." Jed met my gaze. "I should have told you, *me* of all people."

I knew what he meant but it didn't much matter now. What was done was done.

"Good luck at Tufts," he said.

"Good luck at NYU," I told him. "And at the finals. Are you still going to ride after you're done?"

"I don't know. We'll see. We're selling this guy." Jed patted his horse. "My eq horse is a lease. Maybe I'll get a jumper and do the A/Os. I don't have any firm plans."

"Me neither," I said.

# Chapter 39

BACKCOUNTRY WAS PACKED. People lined the walls, the bar, the dance floor. Chris and I had decided to go—one last night out, one final appearance.

"I've never seen it like this, ever," I said.

Chris leaned close, but he still had to shout for me to hear him. "It's the last day. Everybody's here to celebrate, or drown their sorrows. It's like this every year."

The way Chris explained it made it all seem so final. The last day. The last night of the summer. The last time we'd be together?

As the bartender poured our drinks, I looked out over the room at the pool table where I'd seen Chris play that first night.

We sat with Paul and Danny. Danny asked Chris what was next for him.

"Headed home with just the two. I'm gonna see what's what and go from there." Chris still hadn't figured out Arkos, but maybe he would. And maybe Logan would continue to show promise. Maybe he could get them going well by Florida and people would see him and consider giving him their horses to train, or ride with him themselves. Maybe he'd develop a training stable. He was a great teacher, that much was clear, but I knew in his heart he wanted to ride more than teach.

"Sorry, man," Danny said.

Chris shrugged. "Ups and downs. Part of the life, right?"

"I'll drink to that." Danny raised his glass and so did Paul.

I could tell Chris was trying to act strong and that the status of his career upset and worried him more than he let on. "You headed to HITS?" Chris asked.

"Yup. MB's back. She's coming with a few. Landon is coming."

Her name hung there. MB. I hated that she had a cute nickname. Of course she was coming home. She couldn't stay in Europe forever. I tried to gauge what Chris was thinking about her, whether she still mattered to him. You didn't go from seriously dating a person to feeling nothing for them, just like that. I wasn't exactly an expert in relationships—far from it—but even I knew that. Chris and she had been together for a long time. Even if it felt like longer, we'd only been together a matter of weeks. And now I'd be gone, and MB would be around.

My cheeks felt hot. I didn't want thoughts of MB to ruin this last night. I didn't want all the thoughts I'd been pushing away of what would happen between me and Chris after I left the show swirling around in my head. But there they were. And Mary Beth was a big part of them.

I picked up my drink and instead of sipping it like I usually did, I gulped it down, even though the back of my throat stung as I did. My head felt nearly immediately blurry, and somehow clearer of all my doubts and fears at the same time. This is why people get drunk, I thought to myself. This works. At least temporarily.

Danny got us all another round and I drank the next one quickly too. Chris shot me a sideways glance and I told him it was the last night and I was just living a little. But that wasn't what I was doing at all.

He frowned at me and I looked away to avoid talking about it anymore. Later, I decided I better see how drunk I really was and if I could walk. I excused myself to go to the bathroom.

My first few steps I wasn't sure I was going to make it. I thought about turning back, but then I stabilized and felt better. I went to the bathroom and leaned over the sink. I let the cold water run over my hands and then pressed my cool hands to my forehead. I didn't want to be drunk and ruin my last night with Chris. I breathed deeply, picked up my head again, and looked in the mirror. My cheeks and ears were red. What the hell was I doing?

There was rustling behind me and I turned around to face the bank of stalls. I had thought I was the only one in the bathroom, a narrow three-staller with dim lighting and a small window in the corner that was open a crack. I heard a low whine that sounded like someone trying not to cry, but failing.

"Are you okay in there?" I asked. Usually I might have thought more before asking, but the alcohol had made me bolder.

The toilet flushed. The stall door opened. Zoe's face was redder than mine and her eyes were slivers, wet with tears.

"I'm fine. Perfectly fine. Awesome, actually. How's your last night before you never see Chris again?"

"I didn't steal him from you," I said. "So I don't get why you act like I did something so wrong to you."

Zoe slouched, her hip up against the stall door. "Maybe he was going to be that good guy you said I deserved."

Zoe and I stood there in the grim bathroom. I wished she would apologize, but she wasn't going to. I wished I wasn't drunk. I was worried about what I might say. I wasn't sure I could forgive her anyway, even if she gave the most heartfelt apology. Her actions had too big implications.

"So you go and ruin his reputation?" I said. "You know Harris pulled his horses, right?"

Zoe showed no emotion. I wondered if deep down she felt badly at least for hurting Chris.

"And I thought you were my friend," I added.

Even after what happened, I didn't wish we'd never been friends. Zoe had shown me how great it was to have a best friend. She'd made me think that maybe I'd find a friend like her at Tufts, only better, only truer.

"Bye, Zoe," I said, before this got worse and I said something I regretted. I wasn't going to try to save her anymore. Let her sleep with Dermott or Trevor. Let her figure out her own life. I had my own problems to sort out. "I hope things get better for you."

"You know she's home," Zoe called after me. "Mary Beth's home and I heard she wants Chris back."

I let her words drift over me. As much as I wanted to, I couldn't totally ignore or discount them.

When I came back to the table, I asked Chris if we could go home. I wanted to be alone with him. It was the last time, for a while anyway, and even if I was drunk, I wanted to savor it.

# Chapter 40

THAT MORNING EVERYTHING felt slow. Waking up next to Chris, getting out of bed and into the shower. I couldn't believe Circuit was over.

At the horse show, everyone was busy packing up. Trailers dotted the grounds, pulled up as close to the tents as possible. Grooms were loading trunks, flowers, water buckets, and saddles. The rings themselves looked forlorn, with all the jumps pushed into the middle, ready to be carted to the next show. It was a dry day and sunny, with dust blowing up over the grounds from the burnt-out fields that had been so green when the summer started. I thought how different it was for most of the people packing up. For them it was just the end of one show and the beginning of another somewhere else down the road. Perhaps they would stop home or layover somewhere to rest the horses, but then they would be off again. It was one endless loop of horse shows.

Mrs. Gorham wasn't coming to get Logan, which was kind of a shame because I would have liked her to see how much I'd learned and how great I was with Logan now. But Logan was going to Pennsylvania on a truck with Arkos.

Mike had come to say good-bye while I was taking down the stalls.

"I'd ask if you need any help, but you're an old pro now," he said.

"What can I say? I learned from the best."

"So it's off to college?"

"I guess so."

"Well, if that doesn't work out, give me a call . . . I can probably find you a job grooming."

I smiled. He was probably kidding but in all honesty a job as a groom didn't seem like the worst thing to me anymore. "Thanks, Mike," I said. "For *everything*."

He quickly glanced away and it was like there was plenty we weren't saying but both understood—Chris, Jamie, Zoe.

"Don't be a stranger," Mike said.

"Never," I told him.

I took down the cross ties, the buckets in Logan's stall, the bird box, and lined them all up outside the grooming stall. I wrapped Logan and left only his halter and lead rope by his door.

I glanced at my sixth and my long yellow classic ribbon that hung from Logan's stall. I took them off his door.

Chris came over and asked if Logan was ready. We walked him over to Chris's stalls where the trailer was parked. I kissed Logan on the nose and started crying. I could never have imagined how much I'd miss him and how much he meant to me now. I'd miss getting up each morning knowing he was waiting for me to feed him, depending on me. I'd miss cleaning his stall and how good it felt when it was beautifully clean. I'd miss cleaning my tack and raking the aisle. I'd miss coming to check on Logan at night. I'd even miss cleaning out the poop in his water buckets.

"I'll take good care of him," Chris said, as he took the lead rope from me.

"I know."

I wiped away my tears and watched Chris lead Logan up the ramp. I hoped I'd see Logan soon. But what if Chris thought it was best to sell him, or things didn't work out between Chris and me?

If I thought saying good-bye to Logan was hard, then came saying good-bye to Chris. We would text non-stop and FaceTime and talk on the phone. But it wouldn't be the same as seeing him and spending each night with him. And I think we both knew that things between us were uncertain. I was headed to college; he was trying to reboot his career. Just those two different tracks were enough to put us worlds apart. Then there was Mary Beth.

"You ready to head off?" Chris said.

I nodded. I had packed up all my stuff from the condo and loaded it into my car. Left the key on the coffee table for the realtor. That was it. I was ready to go. Only I wasn't . . .

"Not really," I confessed.

"This isn't *it*," Chris said.

But he couldn't know that. For a moment, we both stood still.

"There's something I wanted to ask you," I said.

Chris raised his eyebrows.

"Did you—why did you first start helping me? Why did you want to? Why me?"

Chris shrugged. "I guess I had a good feeling about you. When I saw you in the ring, with Jamie yelling at you, I thought we might be good for each other."

"Have we been? Have I been good for you too?"

"Yes," Chris said.

It was hard to believe since Chris came to the horse show with an owner, a bunch of talented horses to ride, and a solid reputation. He was leaving with two low-level horses, no owner, and people probably still gossiping about him. But I had to believe that in some way I was good for him too. That the fact that I didn't know the first thing about the horse show world gave him perspective he needed.

I tried to immerse myself in kissing Chris, but my mind was all over the place with so many thoughts of what would happen between us and what things would be like when we were apart. Was our relationship only possible here at the horse show?

"I love you," I said, as we pulled apart. I hadn't planned to say it, and I hoped it didn't sound like I was trying to make something permanent before we left. It had just come out. Probably, I imagined, that was the best way for someone to say, "I love you." Totally unprompted and unplanned, just from the heart.

Without hesitation Chris said back to me, "I love you."

In the car, I turned on the radio, hoping to hear MISSION. I kept switching channels and for once it wasn't on. That seemed like a bad omen. Like a sign that everything was over. My mind raced toward the future. I thought about school, about Logan, about Chris and whether we'd be able to make it work long distance. I decided to keep my eyes on the road, as it lolled up and down the hills. It was the only way to get home.

*

# About the Author

KIM ABLON WHITNEY lives with her husband and three children in Newton, Massachusetts. In addition to writing fiction, she is a USEF 'R' judge in hunters, equitation, and jumpers and has officiated at the Washington International Horse Show Junior Equitation Finals, the Capital Challenge, the Winter Equestrian Festival, Lake Placid, and the Vermont Summer Festival. As a junior, she showed in the equitation, placing at the USEF Talent Search and USEF Medal Finals. She later competed as an amateur in the A/O jumpers, winning top ribbons at WEF, Lake Placid, and Devon on her self-trained off-the-track Thoroughbred. To learn more about Kim and her books, please visit www.kimablonwhitney.com.

---

Want to read more about the show circuit from Kim Ablon Whitney?
On the next page is an excerpt from
*The Perfect Distance*, available on Amazon.

# Chapter One

"NO! NO! NO! What did I say about making a move at the last minute?"

Rob's voice was so loud, I could hear him all the way up at the barn—over a football field's length away. What I couldn't hear was the response from whomever he was yelling at. I hoped it wasn't Katie.

I led Tobey out of the barn and up to the mounting block. Behind me, my dad gave Gwenn a leg up onto Finch.

"Thanks, Juan," she said. Even though I'd heard all the riders call my dad by his first name a million times before, it still sounded strange.

As I swung my leg over the saddle, my stomach started to tie up in knots. It was the first day of boot camp, which was what we called the weeks of training before the finals. This was when Rob got tough—tougher than usual, that is.

Tobey swished his tail and stomped a front hoof as I tightened the girth. He was really girthy so I had to tighten it only a hole or two at a time.

"Hold on," I told him. "We're going."

I gathered my reins, and Gwenn and I headed down to the indoor arena. West Hills was set on a hill, with the main barn, two impeccably groomed outdoor rings, and take-your-breath-away grand prix field on top and the indoor arena and half-mile galloping track down below. With all the well-kept buildings and manicured grounds, the farm was insanely gorgeous.

"Have a good lesson, girls," Dad called after us.

The door to the arena yawned open, but we didn't go in yet. That was rule number one of riding at West Hills: *Wait until Rob tells you to.* And it applied to most everything.

Rob had left the sliding door open because the early-September-still-summer sun was beating down on the metal roof, heating the indoor like a sauna. But since most of the finals took place indoors, we practiced inside no matter how hot it was. Rob stood in the middle as Katie cantered a circle around him. Tara was standing on the side of the ring.

Rob stood five foot ten, had rusty brown hair, and was a little on the beefy side. He had great posture—he never slouched or slumped. No one knew his age for sure, but we guessed that he was around forty-five. If you saw him on the street, you probably wouldn't think much of him, but in the horse show world he was basically God. Parents sent their kids from all over the country and paid a fortune for them to train with him. He was notorious for being tough on his riders, but as much as we griped about him, we all knew it was worth it because he was the best.

"How did that feel?" he asked Katie in a deceptively moderate tone. A tone I knew all too well.

Katie answered softly, "Not so good, I guess."

Knowing what was coming next, I cringed for her and for how many times I'd been in her situation.

Suddenly Rob's voice boomed again. "Jesus Christ, Katie, have some conviction! Speak up! It was lousy. You were completely out of control."

Rob paused. The worst was hopefully over—once he'd exploded, he usually calmed down.

He continued in a saner tone, "The course is all parts that make up a whole. You have to ride it in parts and put the parts together. You got going and didn't stop to take a breath or collect your horse the whole way around. Again. And this time, for God's sake, get it right."

Katie cantered off the circle to start over. Her face muscles were tensed, like she was trying to hold it all together. I watched in silence, thinking: *Please don't mess up.* Because the more upset Rob got now, the tougher he would be on me. But also because Katie was my best friend at the barn and probably my best friend, period. If we hadn't met at the barn, I'm sure we never would have been friends. Other than riding, we really didn't have much in common. But horses had brought us together, and we'd found that even though we were from completely different backgrounds, we got along well.

Stretch's nostrils flared with each stride and he expelled the air in forceful snorts. His neck glistened with sweat, and where the reins rubbed against him was white with foam.

All in all, Katie was a pretty bad rider, but she got away with a fair amount because of Stretch. Stretch had won the finals a record five times and was Rob's best horse. He was practically a legend in the equitation world. He was pure white and was so easy anyone could ride him. In fact, Stretch would probably jump a course with a monkey on his back. When you jump, you have to tell your horse where to take off from. The correct spot to take off from—not too close to the jump and not too far away—is called the right "distance." If you're good at judging the distances and telling your horse where to take off from, people say you have a "good eye." Katie had what people called "no eye." Luckily for her, Stretch had a good eye of his own, and even when Katie didn't see the perfect distance, a lot of the time Stretch did. He was also known for being able to make a really long distance look good—hence the name Stretch.

Katie's father was a big-time New York City litigator, and he paid six figures a year to lease Stretch. Many of the eq riders at West Hills leased horses from Rob. Some riders even came specifically to ride with Rob because of his amazing stock of proven eq horses. I, however, rode whatever Rob gave me. For the past three years that had been Tobey.

This time Katie managed the course without any major faults. She kept cantering after the last fence because that was rule number one-A: *You're not done until Rob says you're done.*

"Okay, let him walk," Rob said. "Good enough . . . for today."

Katie barely had to tug on the reins and Stretch dropped back to a walk.

"The one thing I want you to think about is being subtle," Rob told her. "When you see the distance, don't make a big move for it. The judges never want to see that big move. Understand?"

"Yes," Katie said. "Thank you, Rob. Thanks a lot." Rule

number two: *Always say please and thank you.* The rules weren't printed up and handed to you when you arrived at West Hills, but if you had any sense at all, you learned them quickly.

Rob turned to Gwenn and me. "Come on in, girls."

I took a deep breath and tried to ignore the butterflies attacking my stomach. After all, I had lived through boot camp and the finals plenty of times before. But it didn't matter. I could do the finals a hundred times and I'd still be fighting my nerves the whole way through. And at seventeen, this was my last chance.

Gwenn had headed into the ring. I realized I hadn't budged.

"Francie?" Rob said. "Would you like to grace us with your presence?"

*Here goes* everything, I thought, and pressed Tobey forward into the ring.

\* \* \*

*The Perfect Distance* is available on Amazon

Made in the USA
San Bernardino, CA
20 December 2015